Among the Swamp People

Among the
Swamp People

Life in Alabama's Mobile-Tensaw River Delta

WATT KEY

ILLUSTRATIONS BY KELAN MERCER

The University of Alabama Press   Tuscaloosa

The University of Alabama Press
Tuscaloosa, Alabama 35487-0380
uapress.ua.edu

Hardcover edition published 2015.
Paperback edition published 2018.
eBook edition published 2015.

Inquiries about reproducing material from this work should be addressed to
the University of Alabama Press.

Typeface: Scala Pro

Cover image: Kelan Mercer © 2014; courtesy of the artist
Cover design: Michele Myatt Quinn
Interior illustrations: Kelan Mercer © 2014; courtesy of the artist

Paperback ISBN: 978-0-8173-5932-4

A previous edition of this book has been catalogued by the Library of
Congress as follows:

Library of Congress Cataloging-in-Publication Data
Key, Watt.
Among the swamp people : life in Alabama's Mobile-Tensaw River Delta /
Watt Key ; illustrations by Kelan Mercer.
pages cm
ISBN 978-0-8173-1885-7 (cloth : alkaline paper) — ISBN 978-0-8173-8890-4
(ebook)
1. Mobile-Tensaw Delta (Ala.)—Social life and customs. 2. Baldwin County
(Ala.)—Social life and customs. 3. Country life—Alabama—Mobile-Tensaw
Delta. 4. Country life—Alabama—Baldwin County. 5. Key, Watt. 6. Key,
Watt—Homes and haunts—Alabama—Baldwin County. 7. Swamps—
Alabama—Baldwin County. 8. Camps—Alabama—Baldwin County.
9. Mobile-Tensaw Delta (Ala.)—Biography. 10. Baldwin County (Ala.)—
Biography. I. Title.
F332.B2K49 2015
976.1′21—dc23   2014049387

FOR

Bart, Tracy, Pye, Kenny, George, Sharon, Raymond, Glenda, Randy, Jim, Dorris, Peter, Murray, Bradford, Russell, and all the rest of my swamp friends

Contents

Preface

Even though this is a work of nonfiction, almost all of the names in this collection have been changed. I want to protect the identities of those involved, but also, some of the real names are so stereotypical that they come across as cliché. For example, Bubba is the real name of one of my friends in this collection. I couldn't use that without losing credibility.

Many of these stories were originally published in *Mobile Bay Magazine*, condensed to fit the format of that publication. Inspired by the interest in these articles, I decided to present an unabridged version of my journal kept during my years among the swamp people of the Mobile-Tensaw Delta.

Introduction

The air was still cool with the tailings of spring and the sky was deep blue. The river sparkled and flowed deep and healthy in its channel through the marsh. I lay on my back on a raft of lashed telephone pilings connected to a small jon boat. I wore nothing but some cutoffs and a baseball cap pulled over my eyes while my friends pulled me up the river. Sometimes, I'd roll over and hold up my hand. Someone would drop a beer over the side of the boat and I'd pull it from the water as it floated past. I don't remember many times being more satisfied with who and where I was than at that moment on that raft. I was going to build my swamp camp, stay there, and write about it.

The Mobile-Tensaw Delta, or "the swamp," consists of almost two hundred and sixty thousand acres of wetlands located just north of Mobile Bay, formed by the confluence of the Alabama and Tombigbee rivers. It is second only to the Mississippi River Delta in size. It's been nearly twenty years since I first discovered the "delta" and made it my retreat. There have been few weekends since that I have not spent time there. There is no way into this place except by small boat. And once you get in, there's nothing fancy about it. To most it would appear as a maze of rivers and creeks between stunted swamp trees and marsh grass and mud. There are few places where a man can step out of his boat without sinking to his knees in muck the consistency of axle grease.

My great-great-grandfather had swamp in his blood. He moved into the Mississippi Delta two years after the Civil War was over and hacked a farm from one of the most inhospitable pieces of land in the country. Malaria and bears and snakes were such in this place that a man would have to leave his family in the hills and commute until a suitable settlement was established. Maybe I am afflicted with whatever he had. I've never seen the swamp as dirty, wet, and unpleasant. To me it is a frontier. It is the only place I know where gloom and beauty can coexist at such extremes.

I grew up on the coast not twenty miles south of the delta. Eventually the rivers and creeks come together, empty into Mobile Bay, and flow out past the old Fort Morgan and finally into the Gulf of Mexico. I lived about halfway down the eastern shore of the bay and grew up learning skills conducive to these waters.

The man that made our boats lived on the causeway, the road that crosses the head of the bay and connects the eastern and western shores. This man's name was Stauter, and his wood boats carry the same name. He was a good boat maker and a wise businessman. He launched his shallow-sided, flat-bottom skiffs on one side of the causeway for delta customers and sent his higher-sided, v-bottom models into the bay for his customers to the south. On the eastern shore we faced open water and needed our boats equipped with high sides, stern rod holders, and reinforced bottoms. The boats he sent into the delta were rigged with trolling motors and designed to be light for pulling out of shallows.

People on the bay build for hurricanes and the wood-eating creatures that live in saltwater. The thought of catching a largemouth bass or a bream or a freshwater catfish never entered our mind. It was speckled trout and redfish and tarpon and jack cavalla. In the delta, the swamp people are prepared to catch all things, depending on the season. The water is brackish, and especially in the fall, saltwater fish ebb into the lower swamp. The rest of the time, they catch crappie and bass and freshwater catfish and rarer species like the spoonbill.

Growing up I never thought of exploring that land north of the causeway. To me it all turned to rivers at that point and I'd seen plenty of rivers. Besides, I had enough water in front of me to go as far as my little Stauter would travel. And it never occurred to me that a land seemingly so bleak could hide such beauty and adventure.

The second adventure, woven into this narrative, is one of a novelist. I started writing stories when I was a child. By the time I graduated college I was determined to publish a novel with a traditional publishing house, if not to become a full-time author. I had little training, little encouragement, and little reason to believe it would ever happen. Nonetheless, I set about it with a persistence and pace that almost ruined me.

When this book opens I'm a twenty-five-year-old computer programmer living in Mobile, Alabama. I've already written four novels and will write six more before the book closes. All of them unpublished. The stereotypical scene of a frustrated novelist, rushing home to the mailbox every day to collect rejection letters, describes much of my life. I saw New York as a cold, hard wall, beyond which was the mysterious world of publishing. For fifteen years I threw my writing at that wall, hoping to get something over. And hoping someone would see it and find value in my creations. Until one day I had to accept that life doesn't always turn out like you imagined.

I certainly never imagined myself obsessed with constructing a crude camp of driftwood, accessible only by small boat, five miles deep into swamps of the Mobile-Tensaw Delta.

Discovery—Spring 1996

My wife, Katie, and I moved to Mobile shortly after we were married. It was hard for me to make that move. I'd always considered myself a country boy and never imagined that I'd live in a city. But now there were more important things in my life than what I'd not imagined. To make me feel better, Katie suggested we build a workshop in the backyard where I could store my Stauter boat and continue my woodworking projects. One of the rooms in our new house was set up as my writing room.

I soon adjusted to city living. I had my new workshop and a new job and new mortgage payments to keep me occupied. I had my writing room with all of my comforting books, and my fingers were settling into the keyboard again. I even joined a Mardi Gras society and involved myself with other social groups. My mother grew up in Mobile and it wasn't long before I mended lost connections and fell in with the children of her old friends.

My new life distracted me from my old ways for a while, but after a year I became restless for the water again. My Stauter was freshly painted in the workshop and I felt secure in my job and paying the mortgage. The pleasant spring weather only made matters worse.

I thought I would take up fishing again. The closest place to launch from my Mobile house was the causeway, near where Mr. Stauter used to make the boats before Hurricane Frederick destroyed his workshop.

But it would take too long from the causeway to motor all the way south to the familiar fishing grounds of my childhood. I decided to head north and see the lower delta for the first time.

I pulled the Stauter out of the workshop and invited my first cousin Alexander to go with me. We stopped at Mac's Bait and Tackle, another old causeway business that has since fallen victim to a hurricane. We bought a delta map, spread it on the counter, and asked the store owner about good places to fish. He suggested Chuckfee Bay, but I think he chose this spot because I was already guiding him toward it with my finger. Even on a map, it is the most interesting body of water in the delta. Almost in the exact middle of the swamp, it lies ovular, a nine-hundred-acre lake that can only be entered from the south. Around this lake is a maze of creeks that mostly lead nowhere, meandering through the swamp.

Navigating the delta can be stressful. Most places are too shallow to run a boat and the water is so murky that you don't know you're in trouble until the motor starts chewing black sludge and drags you to a stop. After auguring out of that situation, you learn to go slow and stick to the middle of the rivers. You don't know exactly what river you might be on without studying the map carefully, and some creeks are as big as rivers and some rivers as small as creeks. A map is never completely accurate.

But we learned these things that day and made our way up the Tensaw River, through Crab Creek, into Raft River, and finally north to Chuckfee Bay. From the moment I saw it, I knew I had to own a camp there.

I remember seeing a few camps on the south bank, most of them rotten and leaning, all of them deserted. But these camps fascinated me—the thought of someone getting all of that lumber up there and actually building something livable in such a remote place. That afternoon the bay was silent like a deserted party. We idled along the bank and stared at the structures. "I've got to get a camp up here," I told Alexander.

"How do they build these things?"

"I don't know, but I could take that little camp there, jack it up, and fix it. Wouldn't it be the coolest thing ever? To have a camp out here?"

Alexander nodded, but I knew he wasn't feeling what I felt. Not many people do. I was talking about a twelve-by-eight box cabin we were passing. The porch had fallen into the mud and the plywood sides were curling off. The landing to it was nothing but stripped, spindly, creosote fence posts. It must have been years since anyone had been there.

The next day I used a tax map to look up the owner of the property where the small shack was. I was surprised to see how little private land was in the delta. The state and conservation groups owned most of the swamp. My campsite was one of four on the largest of these private sections and was listed to a James Corley.

Mr. Corley was in the Mobile phone book. I called him and asked about a lease. He told me that a timber company had been representing his land illegally for years and he was almost through getting the matter settled. If I could be patient, he promised to have a plan in place soon whereby I could lease from him. At the time, I reasoned that those abandoned camps I'd seen were a result of the legal issues he'd described. But I didn't know much about the delta then and I'd tell you differently now.

It was a coincidence that one of my good friends at work, Carter, had a camp in the delta. I'd heard him talk about it before but never gave much thought to it just like I'd never given much thought to fishing up that way. But now I'd seen the place and I was very interested in where his camp was relative to the old shack I was trying to lease.

When Carter told me that his camp was also on Chuckfee Bay, I couldn't believe my fortune. It turned out that his family owned one of only two more parcels of private land on the west bank. Alexander and I had not motored that far down, so I couldn't picture it, but Carter invited me to go up there with him the next weekend.

It was late in the spring and the air was cool and the sky so blue it made my scalp tingle. We launched Carter's Stauter that Friday afternoon at Cloverleaf Landing, a fishing camp located down a mile-long red clay road, due east of Chuckfee Bay on the Tensaw River. From there, one can cut about a mile off the boat ride to Chuckfee.

I was fascinated by the equipment Carter loaded from the truck into the boat: a Q-Beam, a shotgun, jerricans of gasoline, rubber boots, crates of food, sleeping bags, a duckbill pole, a trotline, whiskey, and a cooler of beer. By the time we were ready to shove off, there was just enough room in his fourteen-foot skiff for each of us to squeeze in. I sat there, feeling far out of my element. I'd always considered myself an expert when it came to wilderness adventure and ingenuity, but suddenly I felt dwarfed by all of the gear and the swamp jungle that lay ahead of us.

I'd only been into the lower delta one time, that day with Alexander, and we'd come from the causeway to the south. The trip in this time was from the east, via river. I sat in the front of the boat while Carter steered the tiller drive from the rear. It was a twenty-minute ride through a maze of rivers that I was sure I would never be able to retrace. I learned later that we had really been on only two rivers, the Tensaw and the Raft. All of the others were large bayous and creeks.

We entered Chuckfee Bay and skimmed down the south bank, passing my shack that still lay quietly fallen into the mud and waiting for me. We passed one other abandoned camp before we pulled up in front of the Delta Shelta, the Carter family's camp. It was built in the same fashion as the others I'd seen: a square, one-room structure, six to eight feet above the swamp on pilings with a dog trot out back leading to a small generator shed. A six-foot screened-in porch ran the length of the front. The enclosed living space was about four hundred square feet, sided and floored with pine planks and covered with a tin roof.

We tied to the dock and began unloading gear. I was still fascinated by this swamp that had always been so close and yet contained so much that I knew nothing about. Even the way Carter secured his boat, simply taking a few rodeo-like wraps around the piling, was fascinating. On the bay you have only a few seconds to leap off the bow and secure the painter with a bowline knot before the waves and wind yank the line tight. Here, the boat sat where you left it and occasionally drifted with the breezes like a leaf on a pond.

The inside of the cabin held two army bunks with mattresses still in the plastic. I learned this was not because they were new but to keep the insects out. Against one wall were a counter and a sink. In the center of the room was a picnic table with bench seats. The place smelled of aged pine and kerosene and the urine of small animals. It was the most perfect place I'd ever seen.

After we unpacked the gear, we sat on the porch drinking beer. Carter told me that his uncle actually owned the camp and that the two of them did most of the work keeping the place up. Carter said he used to spend more time in the delta before he went to college, but now he only made it up occasionally in the spring and fall. He liked to run catfish lines and jugs. I asked about the jugs and he was surprised that I'd never heard of that technique. He explained that you tied hook and line to a milk or Clorox jug, baited it, and threw it out in the bay. Using binoculars, you watched for the jugs to bob or move against the wind, signifying there was a catfish on the line. Eventually, when you finished your beer, you drove out and retrieved the fish.

Carter also mentioned how much it annoyed him when high-speed bass boats rocketed past the camp. The narrow channel running the south side of the bay is not much wider than a two-lane road and passes only a cane pole length from the end of the Delta Shelta dock. I agreed with him that these flashy boats seemed alien in Chuckfee Bay.

Carter told me that Mr. Stauter had been raised in the delta not far from us. His family used to have a farm with cows and a few other animals. They would commute to the city using the boats they built to trade and purchase supplies. I was fine with the part about the boat building and even the part about living in the delta, but I couldn't get past the cows. I imagined them hopping through the mud like horses in high snow. And Carter has been known to get away with saying the most outlandish things with a rock-hard poker face.

"Cows?"

"That's what I heard."

"Where?"

"On Raft River. There's high ground over there."

I took another sip of beer. Swallowed. "Crap."

Carter gazed out over the bay. "You know what I'd like to build?" he said.

"No."

"I want a hydraulic lift like the kind they have in mechanic shops."

"Car lift?"

"Yeah. I wanna fabricate a steel box on the top and fill it with old bike frames. Install it out in that channel. Whenever one of those sons of bitches comes by at sixty miles an hour, I can press the button and lift it into his prop."

We laughed at that for a while. It was soon dark and the sound of the frogs cheeping from the miles of swamp was almost deafening and the bay lay like a flat of mirror under a starry, moonless night. The scenery before me only reconfirmed my commitment to build my own delta retreat.

First Night

After my trip with Carter, I planned the rebuild of my new camp. A twenty-year lease was finalized with Mr. Corley and now the rest was up to me. I decided to enlist five more members to make the expenses easier on my wallet. The first person that came to mind was another coworker I'd known since childhood, Larry Stevens. I knew Larry liked the delta and would be interested enough to pull his weight. The second person I called on was Alexander. Even though I knew the delta was probably not his thing, I wanted him to be a part of it. After rounding up three more buddies, I had the initial six members of the Swamp Camp.

We all donated lumber and supplies and hauled them up in our Stauters. Then we jacked and leveled the camp. After pulling up some of the old dock pilings we replaced them and reconstructed the landing. Alexander even came up once and we spent a day building a small generator shed in the fashion of others I'd seen in the area. This consisted of a catwalk out the rear of the camp that led to a small three-by-four frame structure walled and roofed with sheet tin. Into this we chained an inexpensive Home Depot generator and wired it to a single bulb.

The camp was an art project to me and each load of lumber in my boat was just more paint. While the novelty of it all wore off for the other members after a few months, I remained obsessed with the

project and thought about it every day. During the week I walked out
to my workshop in the evenings and arranged my boat for the next
trip up. Sometimes I prefabricated things in my backyard, just to
be making progress. When the weekend came, I toted it all into the
swamp. Sometimes I had help, sometimes I was alone. It didn't matter. And slowly, the old camp began to stand up again and take shape.

My brother Reid came with me for the first overnight trip to the camp.
It was early June and so hot that we didn't leave until late afternoon
when it started to cool off. We sat on the porch and drank beer and
shot at grasshoppers with a pellet pistol. They are the biggest, black-
est grasshoppers I have ever seen and I've heard them called Lubber
Grasshoppers. I'm sure they are found other places besides the delta,
although I don't recall having seen them anywhere else. The marsh
grass teems with them, and their weight bends the blades and they
thud when hitting the mud. They don't fly and fish won't eat them.
I've never seen a baby one and I have no idea where they come from.
They appear every year like spawn of the mud. I have never heard of
anyone being bitten by one of these giants, but I don't care to hold
them. The one time I did pinch one between my thumb and forefinger, I thought I felt its heart beating between a rib cage. As far as I can
tell the only use for them is for targets and practical jokes. There is
nothing more satisfying than placing a few of them on the chest of a
napping camper and sitting back for the show.

As darkness settled over the swamp we started the generator and
the single bulb came to life inside the camp. Then we got out the
Q-Beam and passed it over the bay. Orange eyes dotted the surface as
far as we could see.

The mosquitoes were out in force and we decided to move into the
camp for relief. This was a mistake. The camp was still missing the
bird boxes at the top of the walls, and the front and back doors had

half-inch gaps around the frame. There were just as many mosquitoes inside as out. But mosquitoes weren't the main problem. It seemed that every species of swamp insect for miles had decided to make a pilgrimage to the mysterious swamp light. The camp, seen from the outside through the windows, resembled an aquarium of insect fury. The spiderwebs in the camp grew so heavy that they sagged and tore loose of their moorings. We unscrewed the bulb until it went out and plugged in an oscillating fan. Then we spat the bugs from our lips and recoated ourselves with insect repellent.

"What you wanna do now?"

"I've got a Monopoly game."

"Can't see anything."

"We can just drink some more beer."

"Okay."

After a few minutes I decided to use the restroom. I had recently built a commode in the generator shed, across from the generator, which was chained to the floor. This contraption was nothing more than a small seat with a hole in the top and a hole beneath it in the floor. Simply a way to get some privacy.

I found that using my restroom was like a taste of Hell. As you sit there in the darkness and go about your business, not two feet from your face the generator screams full-bore, leaping at its chain. And the sheet tin walls only act to deliver this sound like crashing cymbals. But I sat there trying to be optimistic. I finally reasoned that the gas fumes were keeping the mosquitoes away, but the intense heat soon canceled this out and I could take no more torture. I felt around on the floor for the toilet paper and found it. I lifted it and it felt heavier than usual. Upon inspection with my other hand, I discovered it was nothing more than an oil wick. I pulled my pants up and walked out of there bowlegged.

"What's wrong with you?"

"Nothin'."

"How was it?"

"Pretty nice. No mosquitoes in there."

"Maybe we should sleep in there," my brother joked.

We took sheets and sprayed them with insect repellent, then lay beneath them, covered like corpses. I could hear the mosquitoes, hovering over me. Eventually the fumes got to me and I made a breathing hole. I felt predators tickling my lips as I sweated and waited for daylight.

"Reid."

"What."

"You asleep?"

"No."

"Mosquitoes gettin' you?"

"Yeah."

"Hot?"

"Yeah."

"What you wanna do?"

"I guess get up and drink more beer."

We woke the next morning—or rather came out from beneath our insect repellent wipes—to the sound of bass boats tearing by. Sometimes if there was a fishing tournament, the boats made it as far as Chuckfee Bay. With the horsepower they had on the things, I'm sure it was nothing to jet up into the bay, toss a few times, and jet out.

My mouth tasted like I'd been gargling gasoline and my skin was sticky from sweat and insect repellent. My hair felt like greasy straw. I opened the cooler to grab a Coke and freshen up with ice water. There was no ice left.

Our first night in the delta was long and unpleasant, but I was captivated by this jungle, croaking and cheeping and sweating and pulsing for miles in all directions. I'd certainly found a place man was not meant to be, much less spend a night in. I felt like I'd gotten away with something, jacked up over the marsh in our safe little wood box. I was proud of myself.

It was going to be a while before I improved the facilities enough to spend a comfortable night. It would be even longer before I was bold enough to leave the security of the camp and get out into the night swamp with spotlights and frog gigs and whiskey, all the things I'd imagined and heard about. But I was making progress on all fronts. In addition to toiling away on my novels, I was beginning to write about my swamp experiences. And the more I studied the place and jotted my notes, the more I was convinced I'd found a real source of inspiration.

Camp Man

It was soon apparent that I was the "camp man," the person who organizes camp activities, does most of the work, and usually enjoys the facility more than the other members. I came up every weekend, hauling boards and tools and any old gear that might be useful. I replaced the floor and wired some outside lights. I built a lumber rack in the yard to store surplus boards.

"I don't know how someone can like the delta so much," my wife said to me one day as I loaded my Stauter with gear in the driveway.

"I don't see how they can't like it," I replied. "There's everything you can think of to do up there."

"There's nothing to do up there. It's just a swamp."

"There's all the hunting and fishing you can take and nobody for miles. It's like you're in the middle of nowhere when you're only forty-five minutes away."

"But you don't ever hunt or fish. You just go up there and build things."

"I'll hunt and fish one day. When I get my camp finished."

Sometimes I found myself so engrossed in my work that by the time I looked up, night was falling over the swamp. This can be unsettling when you're alone and not prepared to travel back in darkness.

I hurried about the place, tidying up scrap lumber and putting my tools away. I coiled extension cords and collected the trash. Last of all, no matter how late it was getting, I stood back and admired my latest improvements.

I have never traveled the river at night without a knot in my stomach. There are many dangers that you won't find in open water. One of these is other boats. Many swamp people consider navigation lights a hindrance and there's not much law to enforce them. You can run up on a boat as it pulls slowly across the river running a trotline. And I've also had them rocket past me full bore, neither one of us knowing the other was there.

Foremost of these dangers are partially submerged logs, or deadheads. The only way to see these is with handheld spotlights, but by the time you recognize them, it's usually too late. Boats flip, have their bottoms torn out, and have their engines ripped off the transom. I've been lucky the few times I've hit deadheads. The logs were small enough so that my outboard wasn't ripped off. But the motor kicked up and slammed my transom so violently that I cut it and floated for a while until my heartbeat slowed and I gave life its due respect again.

I'm more concerned with getting thrown from the boat. Assuming that I don't hit my head on anything as I eject, I'll be stranded in a place where nightmares can come true. I was told as a boy to always keep my bootlaces untied in the boat. I follow that advice to this day. In winter, you only have a short time to get out of the freezing river water, and if heavy boots don't drag you down, you may have a chance. That is, if the current doesn't sweep you away. I can feel the current in places you wouldn't expect it. My skiff, fully underway, will suddenly twist and move through an invisible resistance like something out of alignment. Perhaps there is a deep hole or a submerged treetop causing an abnormality in the river's passage. Being close to Mobile Bay, the rivers are affected by tides as well as upriver flooding. It's hard to predict where and when eddies and whirlpools will appear.

In summer, I am often barefoot and the river water is cool and refreshing. There is no risk of hypothermia. But if you are thrown out and left stranded in the swamp, you must feel about in knee-deep mud and marsh grass that is over your head. And you know that it will be almost impossible not to come across an alligator or, worst of all, a cottonmouth. Alligators are generally fearful of humans and will not harm you unless provoked. But cottonmouths are aggressive and extremely poisonous snakes. There are thousands of them around my camp and some with heads as big around as my fist.

John said you had a cottonmouth hit you.

I was sittin' on a stump duck huntin' just before daylight. My ankles were in the water at the base of this stump. I feel somethin' tappin' my boots. I shined my flashlight down there and I see its white, open mouth strikin' the rubber.

Get you?

Naw. It was cold. I guess the thing was sluggish.

Cottonmouths will go out of their way to bite you. And I fear them above all other creatures in the swamp.

So being thrown out of your boat is a possibility and a nightmare. At night on the river, I wear a life jacket, keep my boots unlaced, and run with my navigation lights on. I rarely use a spotlight. To me, moonlight and sky glow are easier to see by. And if the night is foggy or hazy, the spotlight is ineffective anyway. Basically, I drive on memory. And I think most swamp people would tell you the same thing. You learn to make a mental note during the day of all the hazards and use this later to steer a clear course. You also use the line of treetops along the river's edge to gauge your distance from the bank. But you are mostly racing ahead and playing the odds. The river is constantly changing and deadheads rarely stay in the same place for long. One of these days, you'll hit something. The gamble is in the river's favor. You just hope that whatever it is doesn't kill you.

Crazy Dan

Toward the end of summer, I MET my new neighbors, Dan and Stacey. They arrived in their houseboat one afternoon and tied it to a hackberry tree about fifty feet from my dock. Their living quarters were nothing more than a ten-by-twelve metal shed similar to something you might find at Sears. It was mounted on a homemade, plywood barge, and the whole contraption propelled by an old Evinrude 70. The husband-wife team planned to build a camp, they told me. The houseboat was only temporary.

They began to visit their houseboat almost every weekend and I studied them while I piddled next door. The first thing that struck me about Dan was his energy. The guy was wired. His face twitched, his eyes danced crazily, and he seemed about to jump out of his skin at anything. But the strangest thing about him was how articulate he was. I did not expect someone that denned up in such a vessel to enunciate his words so clearly. Then I learned that Dan was a telemarketer. It was his business to have an effective, trusting voice.

"How do you even get people to listen to you? I hang up the phone the second I know somebody's tryin' to sell me somethin'."

"You wouldn't hang up on me."

"What could you say that would keep me from hangin' up?"

"I've got my tricks."

"Tell me what you'd say."

Dan smirked and looked away like he would never reveal his secrets.

He drove a Stauter that looked like it had been whipped with a chain. But it didn't run like it. In the same way that a dog can take on the personality of its owner, Dan's boat leaped around the swamp just as wired and strung out as its captain. Most swamp people move about in no particular hurry, taking in their surroundings, seemingly at peace with nature, all while trying to sneak up on it. Dan rides his boat like it's gone insane beneath him. It skips across the water like a flat stone released from a slingshot. And the only thing that slows him down is mud, and mud makes him mad. He hits the shallows wide-open and slams his hand on the throttle to whip whatever's got him. Most people will glide to a stop about fifty yards from their camp and idle in, stepping onto the bow at some point to place their hand on the dock. Not Dan. Dan will yank back on the throttle at about ten yards; the boat sits down and then leaps forward on the back wave into the houseboat like it might go right through.

"What's up, Watt!" he yells.

I've had my hammer poised in midair for some time. "Hey, Dan."

Dan and Stacey fish from the back of the houseboat. They cast their lines out into the channel and prop the handles of the rods and sit back and drink and watch. When boats come tearing by there is a mad rush to reel the lines in before they are run through and cut. This works fine in the early afternoon. But as the day wears on and more alcohol is consumed, the couple loses their edge. The boats approach in a roar and one or both of them will be just starting to stand when the rods bend and tremble for a moment like a passing whale has clipped them. Then the boat passes and the rods spring back to form and leap in their holders, leaving the lines slack across the water like pieces of loose spiderweb.

"Son of a bitch!" Dan yells, straightening and staring after the boat. "Why don't you slow the hell down!"

City People

We always called the cabin Swamp Camp. One day we had a discussion about coming up with something more original and Larry suggested the Boar's Nest. For lack of a better name, we went with it. My artist brother, Murray, painted a sign for us that featured a cartoon wild boar in a rocking chair and holding a fishing pole. We nailed it to the front of the camp and hoped it would take.

Not long after that, Larry and I decided to have our first party at the cabin. It would coincide with what I've always called the Delta Fall Party. I've never determined who sets the date of this party or if there is some formula to it. Also, it's never called a party. You just hear "there's gonna be a bunch of people up at their camps this weekend," which is a statement unusual enough to let you know the date is upon you.

At the time I was only acquainted with what I term "city people," individuals like Larry and Carter who live in Mobile and use the delta for recreational purposes on occasion. They grew up duck hunting and fishing these waters with their fathers and friends and have a rich history of delta experiences. They are by no means poor sportsmen, but they are not experienced in swamp life. Compared to the swamp people, they merely piddle.

Swamp people receive sustenance from the delta. They are often husband-wife teams whose camps are their waterfront property and their second home. They don't just bass fish and duck hunt but are typically involved in more productive activities like catfishing and hog hunting. And they don't do these things to impress themselves or anyone else; they do it because it is as natural as a cat killing a mouse.

The fall party is for the city people. They blow in, bombard the swamp with chaos, and limp home a day or two later. It is their playground, not their lifestyle. But the delta does not discriminate. There is enough room for people to act as offensive as they like and the swamp absorbs it over miles of fetid tangle and gentle water.

For the most part, these two groups don't mix. Swamp people like to be left alone and city people move too fast to notice them.

Larry, who is always at the forefront of several social networks, knew about the fall party and clued me in. Carter was having people to the Delta Shelta and a bunch would be at the Raft River Hilton and the Stud Duck, and Mitch Taylor would be bringing his houseboat up from the causeway.

I invited two of my college buddies down from Montgomery, Preston and Wilson. I was going to take Friday off work and meet Preston around noon at my house. We would ride up to the camp and then I would return to get Wilson later that evening.

One of the most enjoyable parts of having a delta camp is taking someone there for the first time. I've never known anyone that wasn't impressed. But I have known more than one who was only impressed for one night, Preston being one of them.

We go back a long way, Preston and I. We were fast friends in college primarily because he was the most honest and reliable of the people I knew. And Preston also supported my writing when others didn't really understand it or care. An English major, he was now a lawyer. In our school days we talked about books and swapped short stories on occasion, and he offered me the encouragement that I needed to keep practicing.

But Preston has always relied on his comforts more than I have. And whatever comforts you think you need, you won't find them at my camp. Your quarters for the night will probably be the dirtiest you've experienced since your worst camping trip. And if you feel something biting you, or perhaps a strange rash breaking out, don't think you are imagining things. There are plenty of opportunistic ailments to watch for in the delta.

Larry, Preston, and I hung around the camp until late afternoon, and then I left to meet Wilson back at my house in Mobile. I intended to return, but Wilson got in late and my wife talked me into taking everyone to dinner. There were drinks and it was getting colder and that ride up into the swamp got less and less attractive. I convinced myself that Preston would be fine with Larry and went to bed guilt-free.

The next morning we left about eight, stopped and got breakfast at McDonald's, and headed up. Preston and Larry were sitting on the porch when we arrived, both looking like they'd had only a couple hours of sleep.

"You made it, Preston," I said cheerfully.

His hair was cowlicked to the side and his shirt was mud streaked. Somehow, his face seemed thinner.

"You bring an extra toothbrush?" Preston asked me.

Wilson caught the boat and began tying the painter around the dock piling. "Just wrap it, Wilson," I said to him.

"You bring one?" Preston asked again.

"Why would I bring an extra toothbrush?"

"Maybe because I don't have anything with me but what I'm wearin'."

"You don't need a toothbrush."

"What about some deodorant?"

"Splash some of that swamp water under your arm."

"How about breakfast?"

"I left some food up here."

"What about hot breakfast instead of cold corned beef hash?"

Larry started laughing.

"You'll make it, Preston," I said. "We've got some beer. You like *that* cold, don't you?"

Preston frowned and gave up.

Late that morning one of the city boys came by and picked up Larry. They were going to watch a football game at another camp and I said we'd catch up with them later that evening. Preston watched them go and I detected a touch of sadness in him that an opportunity to leave had been missed.

After they pulled away, I got out the twenty-two rifle and began tossing targets in front of the camp to shoot. We sat up on the porch like old men and drank beer and popped away. Dan and Stacey were next door, sitting on the tiny rim porch of their houseboat, fishing. I'd not spent time with them yet, but we'd always exchanged friendly waves and shouted back and forth about the weather and such. The only progress they had made on their camp was a few sticks of lumber thrown up into the marsh. They didn't seem to be in a hurry.

We ran out of beer just after lunch and I decided to make a run back to the landing and retrieve a case that I'd left in my truck. I was back in about forty-five minutes and Preston and Wilson were still sitting exactly as I'd left them with the twenty-two rifle leaning against the wall between them. I tied the boat and walked up the dock.

"What y'all been doin'?"

"Just shootin' some cans."

I picked up the rifle and started to reload it. After a second, I heard a boat approaching and I stopped what I was doing and looked up. An aluminum jon boat with two men I'd seen in the area before, but never spoken to, was about to land at my dock. I walked out to catch their boat, carrying the rifle with me. Before I reached them, the man in the front of the boat leaped out onto the end of my dock. His face was so red and his jaw clenched so tight I thought the veins were about to jump out of his forehead. He was wiry and muscled in the way of a convict and hair-trigger-cocked for a fight. He got right up in my face and said, "I'm gonna kill you, son of a bitch!"

I think I must have gone slack while my eyes grew wide. I didn't know this man or anything about why he was mad.

"I don't know what you're talkin' about," I said, politely.

"Don't gimme that crap. You little prick!"

He was waiting to hit me. He'd obviously been stewing over this and planning my death. I realized that if I said the wrong thing, he was going to break my jaw, and I had no doubt that he'd broken others before. I managed to glance at the driver of the boat. He was sitting patiently, the unbiased chauffeur of an ass-kicking. Later I would learn that this was Butch Dobson, "mayor" of Chuckfee Bay.

"Seriously, I'm sorry for whatever happened to you. I really don't know what you're talkin' about. I just got here not five minutes ago."

"I came by here an hour ago and you were here! You almost shot my head off!"

"Well, I was here an hour ago, and then I left and then I came back. I—"

He reached down and snatched the rifle from my hand. He held it over his head and shook it violently. "I'll throw this goddamn thing out in the bay!"

I was paralyzed with fear, but I managed to shake my head. "I'm sorry about whatever happened. I really don't know what—"

"Ace, come on and get back in the boat," the driver said.

"I ain't through with him."

"Just come on. He said he was sorry."

Ace started to say something but didn't. He threw my rifle down onto the dock. "You ever shoot in my direction again, I'll shoot back. You understand?"

I nodded. He turned and got back into the boat. I stood there until they pulled away, then picked up my rifle and walked slowly back to the porch.

"'Preciate it guys. What the *hell* was that all about?"

"Guess we must have shot in the direction of his camp, wherever that is."

"Jesus! No more shootin'. And the next time somebody's out there about to knock my head off, how about a little support from the peanut gallery."

We went riding later that afternoon and I saw Ace sitting on the porch of a camp just around a little point of land from my place. You couldn't see this structure from our porch and I'd always thought that it was abandoned. I pieced together the targets on the water and my friends shooting in his direction. The bullets would have ricocheted right into his back wall. He watched me pass and he didn't wave and he didn't smile. I felt a sickness in my stomach, knowing that I might already have an enemy with nineteen years to go on my lease.

As the sun set the temperature dropped. We grilled steaks on the porch and retold old college stories. Just before dark, the city boys began to pour into the swamp full force, their boats jumping and skipping wildly around the point as they came into Chuckfee. Before long the Delta Shelta looked like a marina of Stauters and we heard the party clear down at our end of the bay. Gunshots went off like fireworks and I imagined every living thing in the swamp was crouched behind something.

"Ace's gonna kill those guys," Preston said.

"I'm not ever shootin' up here again," I replied. "But that crazy convict's probably gonna burn me out anyway."

"You think he'd burn you?" Wilson asked.

"Man, these people'll burn you in a second. He probably thinks I'm some rich city kid."

Wilson looked around at my camp. "I doubt that."

We heard boat motors starting at the Delta Shelta, and the gun-shots died down. A few seconds later, a caravan of Stauters raced by with men crouched low against the cold and holding their whiskey and beer between their knees. I reasoned they were headed for Mitch's houseboat. I knew many of them but wasn't really part of their group. I waved as they passed, then the three of us poured another drink and started in on the college stories once more.

About ten o'clock that night, the caravan raced by again, minus a boat or two this time. They disappeared around the point where Ace's camp is and we watched after them.

"Y'all wanna go to the Delta Shelta and see what they're doin'?" I said.

"Sure," Wilson said.

We got into my boat and started toward the Delta Shelta. As we rounded the point, we saw the white of a Johnson motor cowling through the weeds. As we got closer, we saw a Stauter that had run almost twenty feet up onto dry ground. The driver was stumbling around, moaning. I slowed down and recognized Vic Allen.

"Hey, Vic. You all right?"

"Yeah," he said.

"You need a ride?"

"Naw. Anthony's comin' back to get me."

"You sure?"

"Yeah. We're gonna pull this thing outta here."

"All right. We're headed to the Delta Shelta."

Vic waved us off and I motored back into the channel. As we got closer to the Delta Shelta, I could see that they had someone's boat sitting on the dock with the bow hanging over one side and the stern over the other. However, no one seemed very concerned. They were sitting on the porch, carrying on.

"What's up, Watt?" Carter called out.

"Not much. How'd you get that boat up there?"

"It was a bitch, but we got a bunch of guys and lifted it."

"Why?"

"Vic ran aground and Forrest slowed down to look at him and Paul ran into Forrest and knocked a hole in his boat. We had to get it out of the water before it sank."

"How you gonna get it home?"

"We were gonna come see you about that."

"I'll take a look at it in the mornin'. I've had a few drinks. Might not want me to put any tools to it right now."

"That's fine. 'Preciate it."

The next morning Paul drove to my camp in a borrowed boat. He looked concerned, like someone who had just woken up and remembered they'd had an affair.

"Watt, Carter said you'd be able to fix my dad's boat."

"I'll look at it. I don't know for sure."

"Man, you gotta fix it for me. He's gonna be pissed. I can't leave it up here."

"I can prob'ly fix it good enough to get you to the boat ramp."

I went back with them to the Delta Shelta and pulled myself around underneath the damaged hull, using my boat like a mechanic slide. Paul stood on the dock and waited patiently for my diagnosis. The hole was only about six by six inches, but it was right in the front where it would scoop water like an open mouth. I pulled myself out and climbed onto the dock. "I've got some plywood and screws," I said. "But I need some caulk. You got any?"

"I think Mitch might have some on the houseboat."

"Go get me some caulk. This won't be pretty, but it'll get you home."

Paul seemed relieved. He got into the boat and left to find caulk. In the meantime, I returned to my camp where Wilson and Preston were already cleaning up and preparing to leave. Preston seemed in low spirits and I reassured him that it wouldn't be long before he was back on dry land.

I fixed Paul's boat later that morning with the caulk he'd found and some supplies I had around the camp. It was really a simple thing I'd done: made a plywood patch and screwed and caulked it over the hole. I wasn't sure if Carter had left the job to me because he was too hungover or if he really thought I was the only one with the skills to pull it off. But I felt proud of not just fixing the boat but being generally involved in the entire weekend. Maybe it was the start of people regarding me as a real swamp person.

Cloverleaf

I spent my first cold winter night at the camp in late January 1997 with Reid. We arrived just after lunch on a Saturday afternoon and the tide was so low that we had to lasso the end of the dock to pull the boat in. That night the temperature dropped into the low thirties and the north wind howled through the gaps at the top of the wall. The generator was downwind, oblivious to the cold, wound out in its little shed against the single bulb it ran. The night outside was ink dark and I couldn't imagine any living thing not hunkered down behind something. We bent around a small propane heater in our frail swamp box and tried to drink beer and entertain ourselves.

We went to bed early, cocooned into our sleeping bags. I thought about a tent, windblown on Mount Everest. But I was proud and lay awake long into the night imagining what an airplane pilot would think if he flew over the swamp and saw the small glow of our swamp box. It seemed impossible to me that anyone would not be envious.

The next morning, I saw what a hard north wind did to Chuckfee Bay. We had to drag the boat about thirty feet through the mud before we reached enough water to float it. I had to clench my teeth against the cold the entire ride back while Reid turtled into his jacket.

While we put the boat on the trailer at Cloverleaf I began talking to Carson, a white-haired, rail-thin, weathered-looking man in his sixties. He was always very emphatic with his expressions and somewhat

bowed up and flared out like he was about to grabble something. I would later learn that he had a metal rod in his back, inserted after a fall from a ship when he'd worked at Bender Shipyards. This rod, I gather, accounts for his posture.

I assumed that Carson was in charge of Cloverleaf, a general manager of sorts. He was always there mowing the grass with his orange tractor or repairing the bait shop and even sometimes collecting your three dollars for the launch fee. I tried to give him my money that day and he refused it and pointed at the bait shop where a woman was sitting in a plastic chair. "She'll take it," he told me.

"Isn't this your place?"

"Hell, no!" he said, cocking his head back. "It's hers."

I took the money to Sissy, the second character of Cloverleaf Landing. I thought Sissy was a black woman until someone told me she was mostly Indian. It would be several more years before I would know her well enough to hear her story. It was a confusing one.

"I'm one of fourteen children but raised as an only child," she told me.

I thought about that for a second. Some type of riddle, perhaps? But maybe not. One can come across some twisted family creations in rural Alabama. I gave up. "I don't understand. How is that possible?"

"I was the youngest and my aunt couldn't have children," she said. "My momma said, 'Why don't you take little Sissy. You can have her if you're nice to her. If I hear you've been mean, I'm gonna take her back.' So my aunt adopted me."

"How long have you and Carson known each other?"

Carson held his hand, palm out and parallel to the ground. "Since we were yea high. I used to come down here with my daddy and we'd roll up in blankets on the sand and camp out. Where all that grass is used to be white sand."

"White sand?"

"You got-damn right."

Sissy owns close to a hundred acres of the best river frontage in Baldwin County. She says she's been offered more money than I would believe for it, but she's wrong. I would believe it. Although the property is strewn with old mobile homes and rotting shacks and oil drums and bridge rubble, it doesn't take much imagination to see how it could be if cleaned up. But Sissy won't change a thing about it. And most of what you or I might consider junk has a purpose. The old crane, for example, is perched like some apocalyptic artifact on the bluff. An ancient Bucyrus-Erie with a boom towering fifty feet over the launching ramp. I don't know of one sane person that could take an eye off the rusty cables that hold that boom out over you at a forty-five-degree angle. My blood raced every time I launched my boat and passed under the shadow of that thing.

I'd explored the crane a few times, crawling up into the cab and sitting on the metal seat. From its exposed perch, the wind and sun had even baked the grease dry from the exterior. But inside, you could peer deep into its bowels and catch the glint of oil and frozen gears. Mostly, it made you think, "Who in hell left this thing here and why?"

"Sissy, you ever worry about that boom fallin' on somebody?"

"I been tellin' them people to come get it for years."

"Who?"

"The people that own it. They used to load barges with it."

"How're they gonna get it? They're gonna have to cut it up."

"Shoot no. They'll just drive it out of here."

"That thing works!"

"Yeah, it works."

One day I came to launch my boat and something wasn't right. It seemed the sun was brighter and the wind was stronger. I backed down the launch ramp and noticed the long shadow didn't stroke my fear. The crane had crept off sometime during the week.

Even with the crane gone, there were still plenty of items to ponder:

An oil drum. They burn driftwood in it to keep warm while they skin catfish under the cleaning shed.

A Folgers can of rusty framing nails and water sitting under a gum tree. Used for tacking the roof tin down when it pops loose.

A piece of capped iron pipe lying in the sand. Carson tamps pilings into the mud with it.

A five-foot-tall section of what looks to be giant culvert pipe. Carson will set this on its end, fill it with water, and use it to hold minnows. The PVC pipe lying across the yard that disappears into the river will soon supply this water.

There is a fiberglass boat floating in the marina. It looks like it passed beneath a low bridge at high speed and lost its top half. The bottom half is strangely filled with foam. I learn from Carson it is a barge for hauling lumber out to the houseboats.

You were married once before, right?

*To Bobo. Married twelve years. Got divorced. Then got back together
    again for ten.*

Where is he now?

He's gone.

You never see him anymore?

He won't come around here.

Where does he live?
Across the road.

Next door to Sissy's property is Blakely State Park. The last battle of the Civil War was fought here, occurring after Appomattox and before word could get south that the war was over. The remains of redoubts can be found on her property. She once told me that they can't cut down some of the large live oaks because the chainsaws will destroy themselves against the embedded musket balls.

How did you meet Bobo?
My daddy and his daddy made moonshine together. They made the best moonshine in the state. People would come from all over to get it and they'd tell us that. I remember their still over in that creek. They had a hole in the ground, covered with one-by-fours. It was down in there.

She claims to be three-quarters Creek Indian. Her face is milk chocolate with freckles. Her hair is straight. Sometimes she wears a wig. She collects three dollars for every car that wants to park, whether they are launching a boat or just admiring the scenery. When she is not there, signs make it clear to deposit your money into a steel box nailed to a creosote light pole. She says she makes all the money she needs from the landing but works up the road at the Shell station in Spanish Fort because she gets bored. She lives alone now in a house she built on the hill a few years back. Carson is her best friend and is there with her almost every day.

Below Sissy's house and near the boat ramp, at the base of the hill, are a bait shop and an old nightclub. Ever since I've been around, Sissy's been testing different business plans with the nightclub, hoping that it will make money. The first time I walked in there, she was serving beer from an Igloo cooler on the floor behind the bar. One dollar. And the menu consisted of a single sheet of paper on the wall that said "Pork chop Sandwich. $2.00."

I ordered one of each. When she returned from the kitchen, she handed me two pieces of white bread with a pork chop between them. Bone on. She told me that the drugs got too bad and there were problems with her liquor license. It was too much of a liability to be in the nightclub business. The sign on the road changed to Cloverleaf Landing Café. Not long after that, the sign was changed to Cloverleaf Landing Social Club, available by reservation for special events. More recently, the sign has disappeared altogether. Sissy claims that now it is used for her own family get-togethers.

Swamp Writer

I still get a graveyard feeling when I pass old abandoned delta camps that are melting back into the mud. These tombstones of good times remind me that my camp and all that it has done for me will eventually meet the same fate. I try to ignore this fact, just like I push aside the thought that I will be fifty years old in only ten years. And I'm constantly analyzing why certain camps fail and certain camps thrive and attempt to apply this knowledge toward maintaining my own.

It became apparent to me after only two years of being involved with the other five members that an undivided interest is an almost sure way to ruin a camp. For most people, the novelty of the delta wears off after about a year, especially when you're married and starting families and new jobs. With weekend football and golf and saltwater fishing in the Gulf and the various overlapping hunting seasons, one has to be either a delta specialist or on their way to divorce to pull their weight at maintaining a camp.

This leaves the camp man in a predicament. Even if he is willing to do most of the maintenance himself, a thriving delta camp always has expansion in mind. When it comes down to it, a delta camp is really about the creation of a good place to have a cool drink and enjoy the view. There is always a deck to be built that would be a better place to drink and get a view. And then you need a screened-in porch to sit and drink and watch from when the mosquitoes are out. And then you need to build a bar inside to sit and drink and watch out the window when the weather gets cold. All of these expansion projects cost money, and eventually there's resistance from the people who don't come up as much as you, the camp man. They are not specialists.

I realized I was not only a camp man but a specialist. I also decided that the older you get, the less time you have to entertain yourself. I didn't have time to scuba dive and play tennis and dove hunt and deer hunt like I used to. I wanted to write books and build on my delta camp, and the two would coexist perfectly. That was how I would define myself: swamp writer.

To be a swamp writer, I would have to own the camp outright so that I could improve it as much as I wanted. I offered to pay my existing camp partners for their share of the materials and generator. They accepted, and for a thousand dollars, the place was mine. They all walked away with money they thought they'd sunk into the mud. I got the swamp camp. We were all happy.

I decided to offer memberships to help pay expenses but allow people to join and drop out yearly, ensuring a fresh, enthusiastic roster. About this time my roommate from college, Steve Wall, moved to the eastern shore from Selma. I was excited to have him back in my life and got him involved in the delta immediately. I advised him of the big buyout, and we rode up there and sat on the deck toasting high living. It was mine, I told him, and he was sitting on the porch of what would be the finest camp in the delta.

"How big you gonna make it?"

"I'll make the first room big enough for us to have three bunk beds and some couches. Maybe a pool table."

"What about a bar?" he asked. People from Selma are always interested in bars.

"We'll have a bar, too," I said.

"I wanna join."

"I'm gonna have ten members. Everybody can pay me a little some-thin' every year to help out with expenses. I'll pay for everything else. You can stay in as long as you want."

"How much you think it'll cost to build?"

"I don't care. I want it."

"What's Katie gonna say?"

"It's an investment. Like rental property."

"Crap."

"I gotta have it."

"Where you gonna build it?" he asked.

"Where you want it?"

"How about right out front there?"

"Where?"

Steve picked up a nail and threw it out into the water. "Right there."

"All right."

This was the spring of 1998. The next week I called a high school buddy, Archie. His family owned a pole company nearby and I knew he could cut me a good deal on support pilings. The next weekend I was up at his plant with my chainsaw cutting ten-foot sections of telephone poles from the cull pile. Archie helped me stack them on Steve's rickety trailer and I pulled them home with the wheels cocked out like something from a cartoon.

By the following weekend, I'd already filled all ten memberships. Then I found myself being pulled upriver on a raft of pilings. And really, this is where it all began.

Hurricane Georges

Throughout the summer I spent almost every weekend preparing the foundation. Most people who see a swamp camp will ask how you keep it from sinking. It's all about footprint. I lay two creosote two-by-eights, one on each side of a pole, flat against the mud. This is called a mudsill. I'll nail another shorter creosote two-by-eight to the middle of the pole so that it resembles a cross and drive the pole into the mud until the cross rests on the sill. Without the mudsills, the camp will sink. In the delta you can drive a ten-foot piling out of sight with your bare hands.

Most of the members came up and helped me in shifts. We waded about in the swamp water where things unknown nipped at our legs, encouraging us to get the supports established as quickly as possible. By late summer, all of the pilings were down and the stringers networked between them. We barged up the plywood for the subfloor and stacked it on the porch of the old camp. The construction was going as planned and it didn't seem that anything could keep me from my creation.

In September 1998 we watched the television as Hurricane Georges bore down on us from Florida. The day before landfall I went up to the camp and tied down the loose lumber and unchained the generator and brought it home. Then there wasn't much else to do but hope for the best.

It was the worst storm we'd had since Frederick twenty years before. Georges wiped out almost all marine structures on both sides of the bay, and floodwater rose well into the streets of downtown Mobile. The damage might have been discouraging for someone who hadn't been through hurricanes, but we were used to rebuilding and realized it was the price we paid for our waterfront life.

It took me a couple of days working at the house in Mobile and at my family's property on the eastern shore before I was able to go inspect the camp. I realized that even if it hadn't been washed away, the storm surge would have put close to five feet of water in it.

On the ride up I saw entire boats washed aground deep in the marsh. Sometimes the only thing visible was the white of an outboard motor cowling through the swamp grass. Giant chunks of Styrofoam floated in the river from houseboats that were torn apart. Dead hogs and deer rocked gently against the bank as my boat wake disturbed them. I wondered what it would have been like to witness those few areas of high ground where some of the animals would have managed to gather. Hogs and deer and rabbits and bears all in the same place.

When I rounded the bend into Chuckfee the first thing I noticed was a large sailboat washed onto a little island in the middle of the bay. Then I noticed all of the camps were still standing.

The water level could be seen on my windows where it had left a brown line of mud. My lumber was gone, strewn throughout the swamp and washed up into the creeks. Most upsetting, yet ironically fortunate, was that my favorite cypress tree had fallen onto the stringers of the new camp. As much as I would miss the tree, that hurricane had saved my camp. Just a year later it would have crushed what I was to build. I don't think I could have been motivated to start over had that happened.

My neighbor, Dan, lost his houseboat. The walls and roof had been swept away. The tiny barge it was mounted on was sunk where it had been before the storm, the rope still tied to the tree and motor cowling sticking halfway out of the water. I saw the rest sitting in the middle of the bay like a sunken storage shed, perfectly level, with water up to the windows. Dan and Stacey would finally have to get busy on their permanent camp if they wanted a place to stay.

As many hardships as the hurricane left in its wake, it was the best thing that ever happened for my camp in more ways than the fallen cypress tree. The whole eastern shore of Mobile Bay was strewn with lumber for the taking if you were willing to salvage and clean it. I'd spent my youth de-nailing and recycling lumber, so it was only natural for me to look at those debris piles like cash money.

Over the next few weeks I hauled truckload after truckload from the beach in Point Clear to a vacant lot that my father owned. When I reasoned that I had more than enough to finish my camp, I began to clean the lumber of nails and stack it. Before long I had a lumberyard of building materials ready to go.

Man Tools

Reid, you're not going to believe what I just got.

What?

Nobody's got one of these.

What?

A portable, gas-powered wench.

Serious?

Dead. Serious. It's like a chainsaw without the blade. You mount a truck wench on the front and screw all this down to a steel plate. Then you chain it to a tree and fire it up.

Damn! Where'd you get it?

Found it on some web site for fireman supplies. I'm tellin' you man, nobody's gonna have one of these.

What are you gonna do with it?

Who cares? Just keep it in my truck. One day somebody's gonna be stuck and I'll haul it out and they'll be like, where the hell'd you get that?

Someone told me once—or maybe I thought of it and put it off on someone else—that the best thing about a hurricane is that it's the only time you can buy all of the man tools you want without your wife saying a thing about it. And best of all, it doesn't end up on your side of the family balance sheet.

"What's that?"

"An air compressor."

"What for?"

"What do you mean, what for? There's a hurricane coming. I had to buy this nail gun to secure everything down and you can't run it without a compressor."

"Are you sure we need that new generator?"

"If we lose power for two weeks, what happens if our other one won't start? Everything in the freezer's gonna spoil. We'll be hot as hell without AC. Can't get the news on television."

"What's all that other stuff?"

"You just let me handle things. You and the kids are gonna be just fine."

It's a man-tool shopping spree and another way that a hurricane can be the best thing for a swamp camp. Once the hurricane is over, all of the lumber and tools and spare window units and generators go straight to the swamp.

You can be a fan of man tools without being what I call an "equipment man." Equipment men are more into lots of small gadgets and accessories. Man tools are typically bigger and more impressive. And the rarer a man tool, the higher its rank.

I am not an equipment man, but I'm unreasonable when it comes to large devices that pull, lift, and destroy. I have at least five come-alongs, numerous jacks, and many demolition instruments such as chainsaws, oversized crowbars, grub hoes, bush axes, and sledge-hammers. "Chainsaw carpenters" need all of these things. Growing up building seawalls and docks and other marine structures, I apprenticed under and eventually became a chainsaw carpenter myself. Some might differentiate this type of carpentry from, say, finished carpentry by the size of the wood used and the attention to the finishing details. While that is true, I separate us by the size of the tools we use and the strength of our finished product.

I am most proud of my jack collection. The swamp camp requires yearly jacking and chocking to keep it level and from settling into the mud. There is no end to the types of lifting equipment that one might find useful. The one I bring out most is a hydraulic unit taken from a transmission lift. While not the strongest of my jacks, it has the tallest stroke and can therefore lift quite high before repositioning. It is also easier to work a hydraulic jack when you are underneath the camp. I have several sizes, from six to thirty six inches tall. I also use railroad and house jacks to good effect on the outsides of the camp. But my favorite is the ultimate man tool of its breed: the auto-body repair jack. This, too, is powered by hydraulics, but its detachable components position it as the winner. Being practical does not always make the winner.

> *Check it out.*
> *What's that?*
> *It's a wedge jack. Stand on it.*
> *Hell no.*
> *Just stand on it and try to keep it shut.*

One of the components is a wedge, similar to a closed robot hand. It opens outward and is ideal for separating tight spots.

> *You're gonna like this. You can stack these pipes on top of each other to extend the length of the ram.*
> *How strong is it?*
> *Well, it's not that strong, but you can make it as long as you want. And it's got these different tips you can put on it, too. And it's got a carrying case.*
> *Cool.*
> *I know. Nobody's got one of these.*

I've only used the auto-body jack a couple of times, but I open the carrying case and stare at it often.

Water Hunter

In late November, the early winter breezes ripple Chuckfee. Ducks and young white pelicans raft far out in the center. On average, the weather is still pleasant, but enough cold snaps have passed to send the strictly social delta campers home until spring. It is time for camouflage and duck boats. Men huddled low with stocking caps and heavy jackets. Gunshots in the early mornings and late afternoons.

Steve had helped me bring up a load of hurricane lumber the Sunday before. We'd set out early that morning, loaded the barge at Cloverleaf, made the long drag up to the camp, and hauled it piece by piece over the mud and onto the deck. I don't think that I have ever worked so hard in my life as that day and I would bet he'd say the same. We underestimated the job and found ourselves with half our load left when the sun started setting. But we had an obligation to return the barge that day and had no choice but to keep going.

The next weekend I wasn't surprised that I was the only person eager to continue working on the camp. But I'd been thinking all week about that fresh pile of supplies and I'd placed almost every board in my mind. The next job would be to put the treated three-quarter-inch plywood on the floor. Much of the plywood had been carried away by the floodwaters of the hurricane, and I had to slog through the swamp and find what I could. It was torturous work, hauling a waterlogged, sixty-pound, four-by-eight sheet on my back through vines and mud.

But that plywood had been my most expensive investment to date at thirty dollars apiece. I found all but three of them.

After lunch I hauled them up onto the floor joists of the new camp house. I was surprised at how square the foundation was. Laying out plywood will let you know in a hurry how good a job you did with the foundation, and mine was as square as could be expected when build-ing on mud.

Late afternoon I was about a third of the way done, bent over my new floor and hammering the squares to the two-by-eight cross mem-bers. I was so lost in my work that I didn't notice I had a visitor until he was practically upon me. When I looked up I saw he was astride the most unusual means of delta transportation I've encountered. It was a Wave Runner. If you are not familiar with one of these, it is a close cousin to the Jet Ski, the motorcycle of the water. But typically these vehicles don't get too far from civilization. I consider them "wet watercraft" because no one rides them without preparing to get wet.

This Wave Runner looked like it had been pieced together from several makes and models. The hood was only partially closed, and what had once been racing stripes and fluorescent coloring was now sun-bleached, grease-smudged white plastic. It reminded me of a football helmet left on a rooftop for two years.

The rider was about five feet eight inches tall and weighed something near three hundred and fifty pounds. He wore denim overalls and a mechanic-rag-red shirt and Hawken tobacco hat. He drifted to a stop before the camp and sat there twitching to keep his balance like someone stalled on a motorcycle with their feet still up. Across his lap was a single-shot twelve-gauge shotgun. In the small, open storage compartment behind him were two things: a rope and three Busch beers in a holder made for six. He shut off his engine and nodded at me.

"How you doin'?" I said, standing and holstering my hammer.

"Ah-ite," he replied. "Gone be nice."

"I appreciate it. What you huntin'?"

"Lookin' for some deer. You seen any?"

"No," I said. "You kill deer up here?"

"There's lots of deer up here."

"How you get 'em back?"

He took one hand off the handlebars and started to turn around. The Wave Runner tilted suddenly and his hand shot back into place. It was a second before he got his balance. "Rope back there," he finally said.

"You drag it back?"

"Yeah. This thing'll ski 'em."

"You shoot any big bucks lately?"

"Not lately. I shot an eight point last year."

"Serious?"

"Serious. I used to come up here a lot more a few years back. I used to be in a camp with a fellow name Ace Crevan."

"I know Ace," I said.

"We sorta got into an argument."

"Yeah. I sorta got into one with him, too."

The fellow shook his head. "You watch out for Ace, now."

"I will. Take it easy."

He started the engine and I watched him relax as the vehicle moved away. I've never seen that man or his contraption since. But this was not the last time I'd be impressed with swamp ingenuity.

Swamp Camp

It seemed word had gotten out that Mr. Corley was offering official leases, and Chuckfee Bay was thriving with at least three new camps under construction. One of these camps was just on the other side of Dan, and I stopped by to introduce myself after a long day of sawing and nailing.

This new camp belonged to Jack and his wife, Carla. I'd waved at them several times and they had always seemed friendly. Their camp was going up faster than some of the others.

"What you gonna put over this plywood, Jack?"

"Nothin'. Gonna caulk up the cracks and leave it like that."

"I told Jack I ain't cleanin' them hogs outside when it's rainin'," Carla said.

Their last name was Johnson and both of them grew up not far from my childhood home. The Johnsons were fishermen; Jack used his father's shrimp boat to make a living during shrimp season and worked as a carpenter the rest of the year. Carla cleaned houses. Their sixteen-year-old son, Hank, paddled an aluminum skiff through the swamp like something out of a Cormac McCarthy novel. Carla informed me that Hank had been conceived in the delta. Of course I wanted more details on that situation, and I'm sure she would have obliged me, but we'd just met.

I knew another Johnson growing up in Point Clear. He owned a small general store a mile down the road from my house. The store closed when I was about ten years old, but I still remember it well. In my mind, its most outstanding feature was the cooler with block ice. We would often walk to "Johnsons" as we called it in the dead heat of summer, when the asphalt was vapory and so hot that we had to keep our bare feet in the fetid ditch water alongside the road. Walking into that ice cooler would almost make you pass out.

So I had some history with Johnsons and felt enough of a connection to Jack to make me glad he was a neighbor.

Throughout the winter I continued to come up on weekends with whatever help I could find. Dan had started his camp next door, but progress was slow. His pilings stood bare for almost two months before he started running the floor joists. Jack's camp was moving along quickly, and I stopped by to have a drink with them occasionally. The Delta Shelta had suffered a good deal of damage during the hurricane and Carter had yet to come up and start repairs.

One day I noticed that the cabin of Dan's houseboat, still in the middle of the bay, was charred like someone had tried to burn it. I didn't think much of it at the time, as the bay is full of subtle mischief. Someone told me once that the best thing about the delta is that you can drink beer, shoot guns, and drive your boat as fast as you want, endangering no one but yourself.

Up and back. Up and back. Hauling lumber and tools and people for a solid year before my new swamp camp was built. I couldn't stop. I was like an ant, a swamp ant just hauling and building. Sometimes I brought guests and we spent the night in the old camp, which we started calling "the shop." I didn't want to subject my guests to much work, but after they went to bed, I wandered about the place with a hammer in my hands, looking for something to hit. It was rumored that I would never relax. That I would never finish. That I never wanted to relax or finish.

My friends were wrong. I would finish, to my relief as much as everyone else's. There came a day when I knew it was done and I pulled my hammer from its holster and let it fall to the deck and sat down and looked across the bay. I had arrived. Sure, there was some piping to hook up and some shelving I hadn't finished, but my creation was complete.

I had never built something I was more proud of. It was a twenty-by-twenty-four room with a small corner walled off for a commode. On the northwest corner was a ten-foot bar that divided off the kitchen. Against the kitchen wall was a long countertop with a sink and storage beneath. The rest of the room was open for couches and two sets of bunk beds.

I was most proud of my floor. About halfway through the construction of the camp, I realized that I had built too low. It was inevitable that I would be flooded at some point. And the pine flooring I'd purchased was one of the most expensive components of the camp and would buckle and warp if water sat on it for more than a few hours.

To solve my problem, I purchased a bundle of quarter-inch wood, the kind that makes up lattice. I ran these strips about two feet apart on top of the plywood subfloor and drilled holes between them every few feet. Then I installed my pine flooring on top. My theory was that the water would drain through the holes and my floor would dry and air out quickly with that quarter-inch gap of air.

I also installed foam board in the walls for insulation instead of the typical pink fiberglass. The foam wouldn't hold water and would prevent me from having to tear out the walls when the inevitable flood came.

On the front of the camp was a screened-in porch and on two sides a deck, part of which was covered with an extension of my tin roof. It was all exactly as I'd imagined it. I thought it the finest camp in the delta.

On a different front, the up and back, up and back of my swamp writing was not experiencing the same success. I was eight years deep in the craft with not even a magazine article to show for it. At times

I felt like a gambler, deep in debt and headed back to the casino for more. Surely my name was all over New York as "that Alabama guy who shotguns crap at us every year." What was I doing wrong? Somebody's got to like *something* I write. Look at all of those books in the library. They all did it.

There was always this tiny voice, a part of my conscience I tried to ignore.

"What if you really aren't that good?" it whispered to me.

And really, why should I be? I had taken only one English course in college. I had no writer friends. I didn't belong to any writer groups. My grammar was terrible. I couldn't get through ten pages of Shakespeare.

But I couldn't stop. I don't know if it was pride or addiction or some short circuit in my wiring that kept me spewing out the pages. Two hours a day. Six days a week. Finish it. Load the shotgun.

The White Car

Some people call Chuckfee Bay and vicinity the south or lower delta. I'd been into the upper delta before, but I've never considered it as part of the same geographic area. It is more river-bottom land than swamp to me. The banks are higher and the trees are taller. Giant prehistoric Indian mounds are scattered within the deep tangle of vines and cypress. It's a fact that some different people with some different forms of entertainment inhabit the place.

There are by far more camps in the upper delta, as the numerous boat launches and higher ground make the area more accessible. The houseboat seems to be the preferred structure. But these houseboats are not nearly as elaborate as those found in the Chuckfee area. They remind me of Huck Finn rafts with plywood lawnmower sheds on them. Rarely are they motorized, and they seem to have only inches of clearance from the water. An updated version of something you might see poling down the Mississippi in Mark Twain's era. Sometimes there are strings of ten or twenty of these dwellings tied to cypress trees along the riverbank.

People of the upper delta refer to the area as "the river" instead of "the delta." They consider themselves river people and specialize in freshwater fishing. They do not have the leach of saltwater creatures that can be found near Chuckfee and other water closer to Mobile Bay. It seems that they are able to spend more time enjoying themselves

with fishing and hunting than the rest of us. I'm constantly at war with the swamp muck and its ill-suited nature for supporting a camp. Storm surges seem to wash over us like tidal waves, but they mostly disperse through the swamp by the time they reach the upper delta. Maybe I should have taken a hint from the Indian mounds and realized that as far as swamp life goes, the upper delta is just a more suitable place to set up camp.

Not long after college, I was invited to an engagement party in the upper delta. My good friend Archie was getting married. His first cousins have a swamp camp on the upper Tensaw and were hosting the event. I have never considered myself very savvy when it comes to entertaining females. On this particular occasion, I was encouraged by the invitation to bring a date, and so I asked a girl from Mobile to accompany me into the swamp.

I'd been out with this girl once before, on a blind date as her escort to a debutante party. We had enjoyed our evening together and I was looking forward to her company again. It wasn't until we were standing in a dark, rutted-out, dirty parking lot at the edge of the Tensaw

River that I again questioned my judgment when it came to impressing young ladies.

It wasn't long before I heard the drone of a skiff approaching us without navigation lights out of the darkness. A man that I knew as Uncle Bob beached the boat and his son, Robert, leaped out to help us aboard.

"That the boat you made, Bob?"

"Yeah, man. Get in. They got the party started up there."

I began to help my lady friend into the boat. "You got lights on that thing?" I asked Uncle Bob.

"Get the lights out, Robert," he said.

Once we were seated, Bob threw two life jackets at us and I caught them and started to help my date into hers. But she seemed to know what to do and got snapped up on her own. Robert shoved us off and began digging around up front until he came up with a red bow light that was taped to what looked like a fragment of fence picket. He wrapped some wires around a loose battery down there somewhere and the thing started glowing. Then he lay across the bow and stuck it in his teeth and we had our navigation lights. "Hit it, Dad," he mumbled.

We raced off into the night, running blind with the wind in our face and the fog slicking back our hair. I grabbed my girl's hand. She squeezed back and I hoped she was doing it because she liked me.

Once we arrived at the camp, there were ten or fifteen people milling about on the porch, eating chips and salsa and drinking beer. I reasoned it was best not to act like there had been any danger involved with the shuttle service. Now that we were on land again, I didn't see that much could go wrong.

I introduced my date to the rest of the group and she seemed to mingle and find good conversation. That set me at ease and I caught up with Archie and his first cousin David and some of the others I hadn't seen in a while. David was the same age as Archie and me.

When I came up to Stockton to spend weekends with Archie, we usually found ourselves on an adventure with David. He was probably the "coolest" boy I knew. He was a genuine river rat, the closest to Huck Finn I'd ever met. His family knew everything there was to know about hunting and fishing the swamps. They spent so much time "up the river" that to find them, it was typical to walk into their empty house in town, pick up the CB on the kitchen counter, and call them by their handle.

"This is, uh, Watt to Little Big Time. . . . Come back."

"How 'bout you, man! Y'all headed up?"

"Can you come get us?"

"We're gettin' this catfish line in right now. We'll meet you at the riverbank in twenty minutes."

Their yard was full of coon dogs leaping at the fence and skinning sheds and stretched animal hides. David had even purchased his first pickup truck with money from the sale of coonskins. He was my hero.

I'd not seen much of David since I'd gone off to college and come back and entered the working world. He'd gone to college himself. Up to Auburn where he spent a couple of years living in a trailer park. He said his "woman" had got up to leave one morning and he'd spotted another better-looking one in the trailer next door. When her boyfriend left, he went over and got to know her. It wasn't long before they didn't need anything but each other, left college, came back to Stockton, and got married. That was a few years back. Now, Tina was standing beside him on the porch and beaming at him like they'd just met.

"How about that white car y'all used to have up here," I asked David. "You still got it?"

"Yeah, we got it. Why? You wanna take a ride tonight?"

I looked at my date, suddenly sorry I'd brought it up. "Well, I don't know if I oughta leave right now."

"She can come!"

"I don't know—"

"Come on! Let's load up."

The white car was beneath a tarp, parked up a wood ramp atop a flood platform. David climbed up, threw off the cover, and there it was: an early 1980s model Toyota Corolla, no windows, mostly rust, dented, and riddled with bullet holes. I didn't see how it was possible that the thing could still be operational.

David got in and rolled it backward and down into the yard. Then he popped the hood and got out to study the engine.

"Go get that battery off the porch, Andy!" he said to Archie's younger brother. "Last time we took this thing out we hit a tree head-on and the battery flew out the front grille."

I looked at the grille and there was a perfect square missing in front of where the battery would have been. By this time Tina, Archie's fiancée, Sara, and my date were standing behind us. I turned and said, "David wants to ride in the white car."

Once the battery was in place, David turned the key and it sputtered and coughed to life. I was about to ask my girl if she was uncomfortable about taking such a ride, but she was already climbing in with the rest of them.

David sat behind the wheel and I sat directly behind him. His seat back was broken and rested against my knees. He draped his wrist over the steering wheel and stuck a cigarette in his mouth. My date was beside me and then Sara sat against the door. Tina rode on the emergency brake handle, cuddled up to her man, and Archie rode shotgun.

Just when I assumed we had taken on as many passengers as possible, Andy threw a sleeping bag on the roof and climbed up top with another boy like he'd been there before. With no front windshield, they lay on their stomachs and grabbed the front of the roof with their fingers curled in above the dashboard. Then we were off.

The white car does not accelerate very fast but gains speed like a golf cart. Even though one of the headlights worked, it didn't do much to illuminate the jungle tunnel we were fast approaching. I saw the flick of a lighter as Tina lit David's cigarette.

"Thanks, baby," he said.

We plunged into the swamp at high speed, vines banging against the car and kids yelling from the roof. It was chaos. I gripped the door on one side and my date's hand on the other and didn't dare to look at her. Suddenly we broke into an open bottom and David spun the wheel with one hand and I saw the feet of our rooftop passengers slide into view as we spun into a doughnut turn. We spun around several times and I could see David's face in the rearview mirror, staring straight ahead, calm, cigarette dangling. Then he straightened the wheel and we were off on another one of the dirt trails. We had not gone far before I heard him mumble, "Hold on." My date squeezed my hand. I felt one side of the car slam into a dirt mound and we were suddenly up on two wheels. Feet appeared again on the downside of the car. David still had the wheel with the underside of one wrist. *Whop!* We were down again and I heard yelling and shuffling above me as the roof passengers repositioned themselves.

"Woodpile!" somebody yelled.

I briefly wondered about the woodpile before I saw an ivy-covered mound in the headlight beam.

"Jesus!" I yelled.

We hit it hammered down, bulled into a pile of logs, and I reasoned that no vehicle, even the white car, was going to come out of it. But the car leaped and bounced over them, buckling the metal beneath my feet, like something plowing through giant Lincoln logs. We came out on the other side with vines draped over the car and leaves in our laps. The only thing lost was David's cigarette. Tina was quick to make repairs. She stuck another one between his lips and flicked the lighter in the dark.

Later on, my date told me she'd never had so much fun in her life. Then we got married.

Carson

While I built the camp not only did I learn about swamp construction, but I absorbed much of the local flavor. And there is no staging ground better for picking up that taste than Cloverleaf Landing.

If Carson was absent from the landing, he was out on the river harvesting swamp creatures. He claimed to sell these creatures, live and dead, to the locals. Mostly catfish and hogs. Minnows and crickets. Sometimes other species.

It's not hard to track Carson. There's usually a trail of blood coming from his boat, up the dock, and into the parking area or over to the bait shop.

Carson, you're always out there lookin' for hogs. You ever see any
*   alligators in the winter?*
Hell yeah!
What do they do? I mean, where do they go?
Them sumbitches wiggle down in the mud. Lay there with their
*   snout stickin' out.*
You ever stepped on one?
Got-damn right. I stepped on one sumbitch that jumped up and
*   about snapped my boot heel off.*

Carson taught me how to say "goddamn" with the proper amount of emphasis. He actually says "got-damn," which adds even more of a punch. And when he exclaims, he leans into his words as if he can throw them at you harder that way. He throws them often. The best advice when dealing with Carson: don't talk bad about Sissy and don't mess with anything at the landing that doesn't belong to you.

> *I tell you what. If that got-damn sumbitch ever steals anything from me again I'm gonna put some of this buckshot in him. You watch me. I know who he is.*

Carson has reason to be concerned about people stealing things from him. His truck bed is filled like someone lifted a tool shed by crane and shook the contents out the door into it. The organization of those tools lends credibility to that scenario.

"Carson, you got a chainsaw?"

"Look in that truck bed."

"Carson, you got a spare fuel hose?"

"Look in the truck bed."

"Piece of iron pipe to prize this trailer off?"

"Truck bed."

"Toilet tank kit?"

"Truck bed."

"Propane torch?"

"Truck."

".22 bullets?"

"Under the cast net in the truck bed."

Most of the time I can't find what I need and Carson will plunge into the heap and emerge with exactly what I asked for.

"Spare two-inch trailer ball?"

"Gimme a second. . . . Here you go."

"You got just about everything you could want in there."

"You never know what you're gonna need around this got-damn place."

Which I suppose is the truth. He is constantly rigging and repairing contraptions to support his swamp meat business or to develop new profit centers for Sissy. I think the most ongoing of these is the bait shop. In all of the years I've been passing through Cloverleaf, I can only count a few times when I might have been able to actually purchase bait. I think this must have to do with Carson's problem irrigating the minnow tanks. A long white run of PVC pipe exits the shop and runs the length of the boat dock and then attaches to a pump of some sort that looks like it has never worked. And the position of this dock leaves it vulnerable to the high water of the river so that sections of boardwalk are constantly washed away, leaving the pump on an island of boards, the umbilical to the bait shop severed and the minnows dead.

The last time I was at the landing, I noticed a new pipe coming from a small creek at the edge of the property. It disappeared into the ground not far from the creek, but it was headed in the general direction of the bait shop. I'm hoping that Carson has found a more reliable system and may sell bait sometime soon.

What the heck is that thing?

What?

That platypus bill lookin' thing. In your boat.

That?

Yeah.

That's the front end of a spoonbill catfish. You never seen one of them?

No. Looks prehistoric.

Government says they're endangered, but I catch the ever livin' hell out of 'em.

Homesick

Dan made the comment to me one day that "he came up one weekend and my new camp was suddenly there."

In reality I had been working on it for a solid year, but my progress bothered him nonetheless. Dan and his wife, Stacey, began to come up every weekend and work. They would come up on Fridays and I typically came up on Saturdays. So each weekend I arrived, another piece of Dan's camp was hammered in place. Soon the roof was on and the walls were up and then the windows in. After that, the rest of the progress was hidden and I only noticed the edge of a curtain appear or a new grill on the front porch.

You heard about Dan's houseboat, didn't you?

No, but I noticed it's not out there in the bay anymore. What happened to it?

He finally burned it down.

When?

Couple weeks ago. You weren't up here. He's been comin' over here complainin' ever since that thing blew out there. Said he can't even get his camp built 'cause every time he looks out and sees that shed it makes him sad.

Sad?

That's what he says. He's been out tryin' to burn it for months.

It's aluminum.

*I told him. He don't care. He just hates it. I finally got tired of
hearin' about it. I told him I could make somethin' that would
burn it down. He got all excited so I mixed him up some diesel
and oil and we took it out in my boat. He climbs up on top of that
thing and dumps all that stuff on it and lights it. Whole thing goes
up in flames and he's jumpin' up and down yellin', "Burn mother,
burn!"*

In the fire?

*Damn right. He's crazy. I had to back my boat off it was so hot. It
finally got to him, I guess. He jumped off in the bay.*

I don't know if Dan drinks more than anyone I know, but it certainly
affects him the most. He moans and howls and crawls across his front
porch at all hours of the night. During the day he's been known to
stand on his dock, completely naked, pissing and swaying with his
eyes closed.

His boat was beginning to look like it couldn't take many more
crash landings. But it wouldn't die, just like Dan.

"If I could only get into that man's head," I thought, "the stories I
would have."

I couldn't effectively explain the wealth of my swamp material to
people back home. Even to my wife.

"It's just the things they do," I told her. "Simple things. Like Jack
runnin' his boat without a gas cap. He just had the fuel line draped
in there. I mean, I would have never thought that would work. But *he*
thought it. Actually, he didn't even know—he just had to do it because
he didn't have a gas cap. I mean—you just wouldn't understand."

"It sounds dangerous," she said.

"It's not dangerous. They just don't need all the crap to make life
happen. They don't need any gas caps. They don't need all the fancy
stuff everybody else has. They don't have to buy a trotline at Walmart,
they just make one. And it's so simple."

"Just be careful up there."

" . . . Now I feel like a wuss for buyin' a trotline."

I could tell that she didn't appreciate what I was trying to get my head around.

"I don't even know what the story is yet," I continued. "It's just all over me up there. It'll come to me one day."

"Have you heard from any publishers lately?"

"Just more rejection slips."

"You've got to be good enough by now."

"You'd think so, but I guess not. I've got so much stuff that I don't even know what to send out anymore."

"You can always self-publish."

"There's no credit in that. Maybe after I get a real book deal."

Katie could get frustrated with the publishing process as well but for different reasons than I did. It took a lot of time away from the family. I'd committed a giant chunk of life to the pursuit, and to think it was all for naught is hard to take.

I didn't tell Katie the full extent of how much material I'd mailed to New York over the years. She knew only the highlights. Even that was a lot more than anyone else knew. I was embarrassed to tell people that I wanted to be a writer. It seemed like such a sappy, self-indulgent, presumptuous, vain thing to announce. Especially when all indications pointed to me ultimately failing at it.

I certainly didn't want the swamp people to know. Even if by some remote chance they appreciated an aspiring author, I didn't want them making stuff up around me just to give me a story. I wanted the real thing. And I didn't want them to think I had any other motive than just enjoying the swamp like them. But the more time I spent in the swamp, and the less likely it seemed I would ever publish anything, the cloudier my objective became. Maybe all I really wanted was to be one of the swamp people. Maybe I just wanted the simple life they all seemed to enjoy.

You seen his right forearm?

No.

Check it out. Twice as big as the other.

How'd that happen?

Said he got a girlfriend in Auburn. He has to drive that old Corvette up there every week to see her.

What's that got to do with anything?

Fuel pump broke. He's got a six-gallon boat tank on the passenger seat. Got the fuel line runnin' out the window and up under the hood. Says it runs good if you don't get above forty-five. But you got to start pumpin' on that bulb if you wanna pass anybody.

That's crazy! That works?

He says he starts gettin' pretty excited 'bout the time he hits Montgomery.

Risks and Changes

Jack and I had our camps finished when an article was printed in the local newspaper about houseboats polluting the delta. Suddenly there was a movement to make all houseboats and camps comply with strict sewage regulations. I was told this involved hauling your waste product out or installing sewage incinerators.

I can't speak for the houseboats, but I imagine the number of human defecations per year on Chuckfee Bay would be something less than fifty. Possibly four of those being from my own camp. And I can't imagine that our waste was any worse than that of the swamp hogs and deer and alligators. But someone had apparently seen some toilet paper floating in the river and gotten worked up about it. They were loud enough to get the local newspaper involved and that led to a reporter traveling into the delta and taking pictures of our camps. Suddenly we were all outlaws.

> *Dan got a "stop building" notice on his camp from the Baldwin County building inspector.*
> *What's he gonna do?*
> *He tore it up. Said the hell with it.*
> *They gonna make us install incinerators?*
> *Hell with that, too.*

Some of the more politically correct groups got lawyers involved, and it was soon common knowledge that we were, in fact, building "barns." I don't know exactly how many barns were built that year on Chuckfee Bay, but I know of at least two.

After about six months the excitement eventually fizzled out and things got back to normal. But the building inspector had made his presence and jurisdiction known and added another risk to the gamble of building a swamp camp.

I'd grown more accustomed to taking the complications of life in the swamp and moving on with whatever changes were needed to persist. I realized that one change I would have to make would involve my old Stauter. It was beat-up and tired from its years as a construction tool. And it was too small to effectively haul the gear I needed for weekend excursions. So I purchased an aluminum skiff, or jon boat, like the ones other swamp people used.

I rolled the Stauter into my workshop and got busy refinishing it. Sanded mahogany and Bondo and Interlux paint brought back memories of my childhood like only familiar smells can. I knew every inch of that boat as I'd probably stripped it to the wood a half-dozen times since I was twelve. This time, not only did I recondition the hull, I replaced all the original brass fittings with stainless steel and purchased a new trailer for it. When I was done, I covered it up and closed the door. I knew the boat wouldn't feel water again until my children were old enough for me to pass it on to them.

My new skiff didn't have much character, but it was as effective as a wheelbarrow. I no longer had to worry about scuffs and nicks. I could leave it in the water and scrape the barnacles off the bottom with a board when they got too thick. And I realized that having a tool of transport rather than a showpiece brought me one step closer to being a real swamp person.

You gonna start it up, or what?
I'm just gonna read these break-in instructions first. It says you have

to run at idle speed for ten minutes. Then you have to run an-
other two hours at less than half speed. And then . . . hold on . . .
you have to—
Throw that damn thing away. You got to run that motor wide-open
right out the chute. Teach it. That's how you break it in.

You put anti-fouling paint on the bottom of your boat?
Hell no. That stuff's too expensive.
How do you keep the barnacles off?
You run it enough, they're not gonna get on there.

You use anti-fouling paint?
I got somethin' better. Cheaper, too.
What?
Get you some regular house paint and dump a bunch of cayenne
pepper in there. That'll keep 'em off.
You ever done it?
No, but I heard about it from an old Cajun.

What's that?
Anti-fouling paint.
How many coats do you have to put on?
This is my sixth one. I think I've got about nine to go.
Crap.
That's what the can says. Carson said use cayenne pepper paint. I al-
most tried it. Then I figured he might be screwin' with me. What
if he was and I showed up with a boat painted with that crap?

Butch

Butch Dobson's camp is a crooked, low-ceilinged, low-light, thieves' den of a structure. It resembles a mobile home jacked up onto pilings, but upon close inspection, it isn't. He's just modeled it after one.

Butch and his brother Trip both have camps. Trip and his buddies in Camp Whiskey Breath, the most remote dwelling in our part of the delta, are mostly Vietnam veterans. I was told once they probably had dead bodies strewn throughout the swamp. But I've gotten to know Trip since then and he is a very respectable and honest man. And he is only about five feet five inches tall. If the Camp Whiskey Breath bunch is responsible for dead bodies, Trip was not involved.

As for Butch, he's a tougher nut to crack. If you'll remember, he was the driver of the boat that delivered Ace to kill me. Since then I learned that he was known as the mayor of Chuckfee Bay. His camp has been in the same place at least since his father was alive, maybe his grandfather. He and Mr. Corley were good friends, and Butch was seen by many as the property manager for the Corley family holdings in the Chuckfee Bay area.

I had never dealt with Butch on property matters as I'd ignorantly gone straight to Mr. Corley. I don't know if this rubbed him wrong or not, but Butch isn't the type to tell you when something is bothering him. He just does something about it.

You don't mess with him.

I don't wanna mess with him.

We set up in his duck blind by mistake one mornin'. He pulled up
*   right next to us and shot five feet over our head the whole hunt.*

Aside from being an intimidating political force on Chuckfee, Butch
was the ultimate swamp person. The Yoda of the marsh. So beyond
me and even Jack that it seemed impossible I would ever be accepted
into "Butch's bunch." I'd heard stories of him swimming naked across
the river with a Rambo knife in his teeth. Being stranded naked in
the swamp and sleeping in the marsh grass. For some reason, always
Butch naked against the swamp.

Though I've never seen him naked anywhere, I did note that he
seemed impervious to the elements. If it was twenty degrees outside
he would still be wearing a short-sleeved shirt and that same soiled
ball cap pulled down almost over his eyes. He has a way of speaking
in short, choppy sentences, with a twitchy grin that's half comforting
and half warning.

I went over there one mornin'. You know those bunk beds right in
*   front of you when you walk in the door?*

Yeah.

They was one guy on the bottom and one on the top. Lyin' on their
*   backs with their eyes closed. Their mouths was openin' and closin'*
*   like baby birds waitin' for a worm.*

What was wrong with 'em?

Butch was sittin' down at the card table rubbin' his face. I said,
*   "Butch, what's up with those two?"*

He said, "I made some wine for 'em. They been like that ever since."

Even if after years of experience I could somehow approach Butch's
knowledge of swamp lore, I would never be able to match his nightlife.

Perhaps I could down whiskey with him once a year and recover. But after he drinks, Butch also likes to fight, and doesn't seem to care if he wins or loses. And then sleep naked in the swamp. I had a lot of training ahead of me.

Regardless of my doubts that I could gain Butch's respect, I made a point to stop at his camp about once a year, just to show my face. He typically had several of his hunting buddies gathered in the camp with him, huddled about some Viking feast of ducks and fish they'd killed that morning. It was always awkward. Like walking into a smoky pool hall in a strange town.

"Hey, Butch."

"What's up," he says flatly. It's absolutely impossible to know what he's thinking.

I quickly realized that it was unreasonable for me to expect that I'd get along with everybody, but I certainly didn't want anyone thinking of me as an enemy. With people like Butch, I was sure I'd always be the new boy. The short-timer. The city kid.

The Trailer Park

There is a place we call the Trailer Park. While Camp Whiskey Breath is the most remote inhabited camp, the Trailer Park is the most remote camp of any description. It is actually only one trailer and sits so deep into the fetid depths of Chuckfee backwater that the word "park" is a misnomer. An Airstream sitting on creosote pilings, so full of bullet holes that it looks like it could grate cheese. So weird that it draws you back again and again to drift before it and wonder who brought it there and with what.

Of course, we've been inside the Trailer Park. It seems that it has drawn many people before us because its contents have been picked clean. All that's left is the peeling veneer walls and old magazines and feces and piss. We've put bullet holes in it, too, but the thing just absorbs them and doesn't give much satisfaction. It's already so molested and beat you can't even tell where the shot went in. Once we took an ax to the door and chopped it off, hoping to get a rise. We got nothing but a heavy door, rattling with spent shot. It rode on the bow of the boat for a while until we could no longer hold it and let it slide into the inky depths of Mallard Creek.

The only thing of value the Trailer Park ever gave us was the bet. On a still August night, five of us in the boat pooled our resources and came up with a two-thousand-dollar pot for anyone that would make it from the Trailer Park to Cloverleaf with only what they had on their

person. My younger brother Thomas was the first to accept. He was fresh out of boot camp at Paris Island and considered himself a survivalist and a man killer. He ran four miles a day wearing a backpack of dumbbells, gobbled salads, and dismissed alcohol.

"Two thousand dollars?" he confirmed.

"That's right."

"Can I have a knife?"

"You got one on you?"

"No."

"You can only take what you have on. It's got to be like your boat sank."

Thomas looked out at the swamp. The frogs cheeped from the marsh grass and the Trailer Park rose dull and wasted behind them. "What about a can of Copenhagen?"

"We'll sell you one for two hundred dollars."

"Two hundred dollars!"

"All right, three hundred."

"Hell."

"It's all you."

"What about mosquitoes?"

"Rub mud on your face. You Marines do that, don't you?"

"There's got to be a thousand cottonmouths between here and Cloverleaf."

"You don't have to walk it, you can swim the whole way."

"How far you think it would be to swim it?"

"Maybe six miles. Maybe more."

"What about alligators?"

"They won't hurt you."

Thomas took a deep breath and looked down at the water.

"It's all you, man. Go for it. Twooooo thouuuusand dollars. Cash money."

"How would you swim the Tensaw once you got to it?"

"I'd get a log. There's whirlpools out there that could take you under."

"How far you think it would be by land?"

"I don't know! Hell. Just get in and get started."

"Don't rush me, man! You even know which way Cloverleaf is?"

I pointed in the general direction. "It's that way. You don't have to be exact. Just swim all the creeks you get to and you'll know it once you hit the Tensaw."

"What if he gets hurt?" my youngest brother, David, asked. "How will we know?"

"Yeah," Eric said. "Maybe he should have a radio."

"We don't have a radio. He won't do it anyway."

Thomas walked up to the front of the boat and stood on the bow and looked out at the Trailer Park. "I don't know, man."

"I'll do it for two thousand dollars," David said.

"Hold, on," Thomas said. "I'm just plannin' it out."

"Gonna be here all night. Just go ahead and sit down."

Thomas turned to David. "You gonna do it?"

"I'm thinkin' about it."

We went on like that for another thirty minutes. Thomas and David did finally sit down and the deal was off. Afterward, I was glad.
I'd gotten nervous about what I'd started ten minutes into the bet. I
imagined what my parents would say if they learned Thomas had died
of snake bite on a wager I'd made with him.

Thomas was silent on the boat ride back. I couldn't tell what was
bothering him more, the two thousand dollars or the Marine who
stayed in the boat.

When we got to the camp, we sat on the deck and had a few beers.
At some point I gave Thomas another challenge.

"Hey, Thomas, I'll bet I can swim from here to the other side of
Chuckfee faster than you can."

Thomas jumped up. "You're on!"

"Sit back down. Not right now. Let me finish my drink."

"Come on."

"Would you swim it or jump through the mud?" I asked.

"How deep is it?"

"Except for the channel, it probably won't get more than three feet.
And that channel's only about ten feet wide."

"I'll swim it. It'd be faster. Can't be more than half a mile."

"Sit back down," I said again. "We'll go in a minute."

Thomas sat down and rubbed his thighs anxiously. "You sure you
don't want one of these beers?" I asked him.

"No thanks."

I sipped on my beer until it was gone. Thomas left to pee and I got
another one while he wasn't looking.

"You gonna swim Chuckfee, Watt?" Reid asked me.

"Hell no. Even if I thought I could beat him across, I wouldn't
swim this thing. Where would you get out on the other side? It's just
marsh."

"He'll do it. He's ready."

"I *know* he is."

Thomas came back and sat down next to me. "You ready?"

"Crap! Will you let me finish my beer?"

Eventually, after I'd had a few more beers, he fell asleep in his chair. Then he got up and disappeared into the bunkhouse.

The next morning, I lay in my bunk staring at the underside of the bed above me. Most people were awake, but no one wanted to move. "Thomas?"

"What?"

"What happened to you last night?"

I heard him sit up in bed. "You wussed out is what happened!"

"I was ready to go and found you asleep in your chair."

"You're so full of it."

"I told you after I finished that beer I was ready. I'd have kicked your ass across that bay. I thought you were a Marine."

It never pays off to bet your older brother.

Man Talk

When I get back from a delta trip with a bunch of buddies, my wife never fails to ask me what we talked about. I tell her that I don't remember. "Nothin' much. Just man talk."

She seems to think that I'm keeping secrets when the truth is that I *don't* remember most of it. All of the talk was shallow and worthless. It was just man talk.

Women don't seem to have anything equivalent to man talk. By my observations, a group of southern females talk about their men or other females. This is information they think is important and it helps guide them in their personal lives. Whereas men will spend most of their social time telling the same story over and over again or making statements that have no deep meaning. And occasionally, man talk involves challenges.

It is common knowledge that although one can go on and on challenging, it is not necessary to accept the challenge.

"Let's go burn one of those rotten camps down."

"How about the Trailer Park?"

"Naw, we like the Trailer Park. Thing won't burn anyway."

"What about the old A-frame?"

"You gonna pour gas on it?"

"We could."

"What if somebody sees it?"

"Who cares? It looks like crap."

"Might catch the swamp on fire."

"You ever burned a sponge?"

"Swamps can burn."

"Whatever."

"You're sayin' a swamp won't burn?"

"Yes. I am."

"You don't think there's anything in a swamp that will burn?"

"I didn't say that."

"You said . . ."

.

.

.

.

"Let's burn the sailboat. I'm tired of lookin' at it."

"Okay."

"Where you goin'?"

"To burn the sailboat. Come on, Connor."

Sometimes, though, the challenges are accepted. We got some oil and some gasoline and loaded the skiff with two more spectators. The rest of the campers, about five of them, remained on the porch watching us motor the hundred yards to the small island where the sailboat was beached. The night was still and cool and cloudless.

"I've been lookin' at that thing for five years."

"I don't think the water's deep enough to get up to it."

"You just stay there on the bow, Connor. I'll get you close enough."

Of course, I had every intention of letting my young cousin Connor burn the thing. I was too old for more than instigation. "That's right, put some oil in there. It'll keep the fire hot."

"You think it'll burn to the ground?"

"I saw a metal houseboat that burned to the water line. Things up here burn."

We hit the shallows and I twisted the tiller and gave the engine gas so that we chewed in closer. Connor stood up with his fuel and got ready. After a minute, we were as close as we'd get and he jumped off and stuck in the mud up to his knees.

"Damnit!" he said.

"Stop bitchin' and get up there to it."

"You better not leave me out here."

"How am I gonna leave without you to push us back out?"

"Crap," Connor said as he trudged up toward the sailboat.

We watched while he walked around the vessel and soaked it thoroughly. Then he backed off and started striking at a matchbook and throwing the matches at it. Finally he hit the right spot and the fiberglass hulk whooshed into a fireball. Connor tossed the gas can at us and leaped back at the skiff while we put our hands in front of our faces to shield the heat. "Go!" he yelled.

"Start pushin'!"

The people back on the camp porch began yelling and cheering across the bay while Connor shoved us through the mud to deeper water. Before long, we were away from the heat and blinding maelstrom of fire.

I must admit, once we turned to gaze at our creation, I was proud. There's nothing like a good fire. Back at the camp, we drank beer under the stars and watched the boat burn silently late into the night.

Several weeks later, I went out to the island alone to see what was left of my old nuisance. There was a neat set of marine hardware on the charred ground blocking out the shape of a sailboat.

Catching Alligators

One evening I motored over to Butch's camp to make my annual appearance. As usual, I walked up onto his porch amid a group of strangers deep into man talk. They grew silent and nodded to me in a half-welcoming, half-weird kind of way, and I sat quietly in a lawn chair against the wall. I was soon forgotten and they resumed their conversation.

That evening Butch mentioned something about catching alligators.

"You catch alligators?" I interrupted.

They stopped and Butch looked over at me. I think it was the first question I'd ever asked him.

"I've been catchin' alligators since I was a kid," he said.

"With your hands?"

Butch made a claw with his hand and thrust it at the deck. "Grab 'em right behind the neck. They won't hurt you."

"What's the biggest one you've caught?"

I don't remember what he said, but it was impressive. The next weekend I used Connor to test the technique as it had been described to me. I presented it to him as if I'd done it a hundred times myself.

"With your hands!" he said.

"There's nothin' to it. They won't hurt you."

"How big do you grab 'em?"

"Just little ones."

"What's little to you?"

"You know, a two-footer."

"Hell."

"Serious. Just grab it behind the neck."

Connor had a few drinks in him. And Reid was there to encourage him further. We eventually had him lying on his stomach on the bow of the boat as we drifted up to a small alligator. Reid held the Q-Beam on the target while I sat at the stern and used the engine noise to drown my laughter. Connor reached down and I saw his arm begin to wave wildly and knock into the boat. Then he turned over onto his back and had the alligator in the air. I was crying. Reid was doubled over. Even though he was laughing with the rest of us, Connor must have sensed that he'd been had. He stood with the reptile and began to threaten us with it, chasing us around the small jon boat and jabbing its snout at our faces.

"Connor! Damnit!" I yelled.

Then the alligator began to twist and flip about. Connor couldn't hold it and dropped it into the boat. I climbed onto the motor. Reid ran to the front. Connor stood up on the gunwales, tilting the boat onto its side, and we all went into the swamp.

All I could think was, "Where's momma alligator? Babies got mamas." I've never climbed back into a boat so fast in my life.

Connor laid down rule number one of alligator catching that night: the person who catches the alligator has the option of letting it loose in the boat. Which I don't have a problem with; it only adds to the excitement. There have been many other rules, but most of these were shouted after the fact, under threat of alligator, and soon forgotten.

What's wrong with your hand?
We were jumpin' on alligators last night and I tried to get a mullet.
Damn. Fin you?
Yeah. Right in the palm.
You catch it?
No.

Anything goin' on at their camp tonight?
I just came from over there. They went out in that Go-Devil and slipped up on this big old alligator they thought was dead. Somebody poked at him with a paddle. Sumbitch flipped around and bit the boat. Their eyes are still wide. Sittin' around not talkin' much.

We met this fellow on the causeway. He had a stretch RV. Said he was from Tennessee and did we know where he could get some alligators. We said what for. He said he had a big old pond he'd just built and wanted to stock it full. Said he'd pay a hundred dollars apiece for gators. We looked at each other. We told him we'd be back later. We set out in a Stauter with a crocus sack. Wouldn't you know it started thunderin' and lightnin' like nothing we'd ever seen. We'd caught all the alligators we wanted all summer and that day we could hardly find any. But we got back late that evenin' with eight little ones and one four-footer. His RV was still sittin' in the same place and he waved us inside like we were makin' some kind of drug deal. We walked to the back and shook those alligators out of the sack into his shower. He pulled out a big wad of cash and thumbed seven one-hundred-dollar bills at us. Then he said he was gonna give us three hundred for the big one.

Thousand dollars for eight alligators?

Thousand dollars.

Damn.

And I figure every one of 'em died in the first freeze.

Kitchen Music

If I were to describe the most likely summer schedule at the swamp camp, it would start with a late afternoon arrival. We'd unpack our gear and lug the beer coolers onto the porch. Guests will be about two beers into the afternoon and settle into chairs to work on number three. I'll begin to piddle about the place, making sure that things are in order: filling the generator with gas and checking the oil, looking about for any wasps to kill, taking the cover off the grill, restacking some boards, and so on.

When I'm done with my preparations, I'll sit down and start on my third beer and stare out over the bay. Five minutes later I'll be restless again and it's time to run a catfish line or go swimming and we'll all take one or two boats and head out.

About dark we'll get back to camp and I'll start the generator and turn on some country music. We typically listen to the same thing over and over. For a while we were stuck with a Wynonna Judd tape. Then we had a mixed CD that began with Rosanne Cash's "Seven Year Ache" and progressed with Willie Nelson and Johnny Cash and finally into Conway Twitty. Every time it kicked on at least one person would mumble a complaint.

Someone will be in charge of seasoning the steaks and someone else with starting the grill. I'm the cook by default, but occasionally

someone else will jump to the task. Then I'm left piddling again, which is what I enjoy most.

We eat on paper plates and pour our drinks into Solo cups. If we're lucky, someone will have thought to bring a bag of salad and we'll pour the dressing straight into the bag, shake it, and pour the soggy leaves onto our plates. Most times we're not lucky. Typically meat and sometimes bread is the meal.

After dinner, some are starting to get lazy from the beer. Those who want to make the most of the night mix a whiskey drink and start talking about catching alligators. The others are eventually persuaded to carry the beer cooler and tag along.

After a successful alligator hunt, we'll most likely go swimming in the river, floating with life jackets and boat cushions between our legs and holding our beers above the water. A lot of man talk takes place.

Back at the camp, those who were slow getting in the boat before now want to go to sleep. Depending on the crowd, it's time for either a card game or kitchen music. Not being much of a card player, I'm usually gathering the skillet, can opener, propane bottle, ball peen hammer, and any other potential music maker. I'm familiar with most people's preferences as I hand out the instruments. Those who have not made kitchen music before are allowed to choose from the pile of leftovers or dig around the camp for something more suitable.

Kitchen bands are most successful when accompanied with country music. It's easier to keep time to the slower beat. We've found that Waylon Jennings songs have just the right amount of bass and that most people know the words. The can opener, my personal preference, ratchets out a smooth tap when played against the knee. My brother likes the hammer skillet, which is a more delicate instrument. Anyone who plays the hammer skillet must be considerate of others and not overpower the harmony. You must separate the handler of the ball peen hammer and the player of the propane bottle as the two don't mix. Ball peens go nicely with a block of wood while the steel propane bottles need the touch of a light kitchen spoon. And there is always someone who will want to blow on the rim of his beer bottle because he thinks it fits the occasion.

Some bend low to the deck playing their instruments, biting their bottom lip, concentrating on the rhythm, and trying their best to keep time. Some lean back and sing "Cruel Hearted Woman" to the cypress boughs. Others keep a steady beat and look from face to face, seeking approval. And there are still more who sit and stare blankly, wanting to slip off to bed but are not quite sure how to make an exit.

Most nights there is a bed for everyone if you include the sofas, but I have seen nights where people are forced to sleep on the floor. I've also seen nights where people sleep on the floor for no reason. On a good night, I will remember to put more gas into the generator before we turn in. This is important since I'm the only person that has any sense of when the generator is going to run out of fuel. On a bad night, it will. And usually at about four in the morning. I'm tuned to the generator's health like a mother is to her baby. I can be in a drugged sleep, smothered beneath a pile of blankets, with no thought of waking, and the distant, guttural coughing of that starving machine yanks my eyes open. The fans stop and the air conditioner falls silent. Everything is silent. I can hear the frogs again. No one moves. Everyone feigns sleep. And I dread the dead thing out there in the dark, in the tin-popping heat of the generator shed. I lie there hoping the bunk room will stay cool just long enough to finish my sleep.

The heat slips in over the next thirty minutes. Bodies exhume themselves from sleeping bags one by one. No one speaks. No one volunteers. Mosquitoes, once defeated, begin to settle on our heat patterns. Someone gets up and walks outside to pee. More mosquitoes float in. The person returns, eyes still closed, and falls back on top of his bed.

The sun begins to pour through the windows turning the heat up another notch. Finally, someone says, "Damnit." No one moves to help him.

People rise early. They wander about without speaking, licking their lips and patting their cowlicked hair. They search through coolers for anything but beer. If they are lucky, they'll find a Coke floating in the melted ice water. Most will not. Most will sit quietly and stare while I begin to pick up trash and toss the old steak pieces into the water.

Sometimes I will start cooking pancakes. It takes a while to get the skillet just right and the first batch is typically made up of vegetable oil sponges. But they're eaten without complaint. And bite by slow bite, our consciousness slowly returns.

Soon the front porch is filled with man talk again, each person reminding the others of something so and so did the night before. Making sure these memories are stamped and filed.

Connor was hell on the fork coffee pot last night.
Who was it that had the ax handle bucket?
That was James.
Idiot.

Where did Pete slip off to last night?

He slept on the floor until he got hot.

Hell, it was hot everywhere. What's wrong with the AC?

Watt forgot to put gas in the generator.

You could have gotten up and put gas in it.

Crap.

At least I brought gas.

I got your gas.

Jesus! Get away from me!

. . .

And then we load up and depart. One more trip logged.

Football

One of the main adventures at the camp is a ride down Chicory Creek. Besides Oak Bayou and the entrance off Raft River, this is the only possible way out of Chuckfee. I say possible because there are times when it is so narrow and shallow and choked with swamp grass that you don't think there's any way to navigate its mile-long snaking path to Grand Bay.

The journey from one end of Chicory to the other always reminds me of the Jungle Cruise at Disney World. In fact, we sometimes refer to the adventure as "taking the Jungle Cruise." Bass boats can't get in there, only small jon boats like my own. The water is typically clear and tea colored over the waving swamp grass. Bass and bream and mullet corral at the bow of the boat. I've seen more wild hogs on this creek than anyplace else in the swamp. They stare at you in disbelief as if they've never seen a human being. In the spring the banks are so loud with frogs and baby alligators that it makes me wonder if the creek might not be the nursery for the entire ecosystem.

Navigating the creek is such a challenge that one's skill for it carries bragging rights. Unfortunately, Steve never developed this skill. I think his problems lay with the fact that his boat was bigger than ours and underpowered. Regardless, it was a regular routine for him to want to take his boat on the journey, partly because it seated more

people but mostly because he was from Selma and drank more than the rest of us.

Finesse is the key to navigating Chicory. You cannot bull your way through the grass and muck. You must keep the foot of your motor in the narrow channels when you have them. Then, when you don't and your propeller wraps grass like a fork in spaghetti, you must stop. You can only get your boat out by quick thrusts in reverse. Steve's technique was to hammer down and, when stuck, hammer down more. After continuously overheating, bending his aluminum propellers, and running out of gas, I thought he would learn that you can't strong-arm Chicory Creek. But Steve's drinking and finesse don't mix, and his solution to making it to Grand Bay lay elsewhere. He purchased a case of plastic propeller blades, something I'd never seen before. They were highly recommended by one of Steve's friends. According to Steve, he could swap them like tires at NASCAR and slice his way to Grand Bay. As I predicted, it didn't work. I still have one of the propellers on the wall in the camp. It is bladeless and smooth like a toilet paper roll.

We would return from Chicory and tie up our boats, still hot and steaming and pasted with grass and mud. We usually had a big crew in those days, six or seven of us at times. Not counting the occasional cooler full of live alligators we'd plucked from the grass and brought back for entertainment.

One evening in the early fall, we returned from a jungle cruise and lugged the cooler onto the screen porch. With us was an ex–football player from the University of Alabama. He was drunk and loud and wet from at least one slip into the swamp. Sometimes newcomers to the delta get like that when they realize they haven't had so much freedom from the law since they were children. Toss in boats and guns and whiskey and a jungle full of animals. Show them how to grab alligators behind the neck and act like Steve Irwin. It was more than our football player could handle.

Once I turned on the country music and we settled into chairs on the porch, Football began to grow weary of leading the charge. His voice was hoarse and his wounds from falling were throbbing and pouring more alcohol down his throat was only weighing him down. He sat next to the cooler, pulled out a small alligator, and began to sympathize with it. He called it "Little Gaita." Over and over and over again. He was oblivious to everyone around him. All of his sins suddenly heavy. He put his hand up to the alligator's mouth and began to stroke its nose. With a quick pop of its head, Little Gaita clamped down between Football's thumb and forefinger. Football leaped from his chair and screamed. The alligator dropped to the floor and scampered into the corner. Football looked at his hand and then held it out to me. An arc of teeth marks like a hundred pinpricks circled the top of his hand. "He bit me!" Football said in disbelief. "Jesus Christ, he bit me!"

"You'll be okay," I said.

He looked at his hand again. "But it stings!"

The rest of the group was laughing. A few were trying to retrieve the alligator from the corner, using a dishrag for protection. "It's hardly anything at all," I said to Football.

"Do you have somethin' I can put on it?"

"It's alright."

"Come on, man! I just got bit by an alligator."

I shook my head and got up and went inside. Football followed. I got a can of insect repellent off the bar and gripped it so that the label was covered. Football held out his hand and I made two generous passes over it.

"Whoa!" he yelled. "That stings!"

"Means it's workin'."

He studied the hand. Looked back at me. "Thanks," he said.

It's all mental skills when it comes to alligators.

Late-Night Visitors

I decided that I would stay a night alone at the camp. It was late fall and everyone, including my wife, was getting ready for the Iron Bowl. Never one to be concerned about football, I took my laptop computer and set out for the swamp to see if the isolation and eeriness of Chuckfee Bay alone would be a catalyst to my writing.

I arrived about an hour before dark and began to piddle immediately. I finished nailing down some decking boards, started a trash fire, and reorganized the tool shelf. Then as the sun began to set, I cranked the generator and unloaded the rest of my things from the boat.

I had a can of Dinty Moore beef stew, a jug of water, and an iced-down six-pack of beer for when I was through writing. I ate the beef stew cold from the can and chased it with some water. Most anything will taste good to me at a camp, but beef stew should be heated or it stays in your mouth and your imagination like the meat and lard that it is.

Once I finished supper, I realized that there was not much left to do but write. The sun had set and the swamp was without another light for miles. I knew I was alone up there, but I kept trying to talk myself into believing that a boat would probably pass at any moment. For safe measure, I locked the doors and shut the blinds and cut the top off a water jug to piss in.

Writing would not come as easy as procrastination. I paced and piddled. Dumped out a stack of cards and counted them. Read a few pages of Faulkner. Took a wire brush to the stove top. Looked at the beer in the cooler and shut the lid against it.

Finally, about ten o'clock, I sat down and turned on the laptop. I forced myself to start and before long I was pecking away.

It must have been close to midnight when the distant drone of a boat coming up the bay stopped my fingers. I stared at the wall and listened, wondering who would be out so late. And then suddenly feeling vulnerable, my little box of light the only thing for miles. A scene from *Deliverance* had crossed my mind more than once. And I had not dared to bring a firearm up since my encounter with Ace.

The boat ran into the shallows in front of my camp wide-open, the motor making the loud guttural noise of one kicked up and spewing mud. In a few seconds, the sound became muffled and I could tell the foot of the motor was back in the mud, bucking and auguring them closer.

"Waakey!" I heard someone yell.

I slammed my laptop shut and slid it under the couch.

"Waakeeeey!" the yell came again.

I stood and began to pace the room. "Who in hell is that!" I thought to myself. "Midnight. Out here. They don't even know my name."

"Waakeeey!"

"Crap!" I thought.

The boat hit the dock and I felt the camp rock. The motor shut off and there was clanking and banging and cursing. Finally, footsteps on the dock and the sound of a cooler with ice swishing in it. I could tell there were two people, and I couldn't think of even one person in the world that would be coming to visit me. I took a deep breath and stood in the center of the room, waiting for the knock. The door suddenly flew open and wood splinters jumped from the frame. Ace stumbled in and pulled Dan behind him at the other end of the cooler. When

Ace caught his balance, he looked at me and howled, "Waakeey!"

"Hey, Ace," I said.

"I knew somebody'd be up to drink with," he replied as he looked around the room.

I started to offer them a seat, but Dan dropped his end of the cooler and walked past us, using Ace's shoulder as a prop. He stumbled over the armrest of the love seat and collapsed with his face turned up at the ceiling and eyes closed.

Dan didn't seem to interest Ace. He dragged the cooler to the front of the sofa and sat down. "Have a seat," he said to me.

I walked past Dan and sat on the other side of Ace. "Get you a beer," he said.

I stood again and began to walk to my little cooler with the six-pack. "Siddown," he said.

I sat again and he flipped open the lid to his own cooler and began to hit his hand bluntly against the ice. Finally he came out with a Budweiser and threw it onto the sofa next to me. Then he managed to get one for himself and he opened it and sat back.

"Where'd y'all come from?" I asked him.

"Liz's."

For people that head into the swamp from the causeway, Liz's Haven is the most notorious launching spot. Some might consider it the gateway to the delta. It consists of a small, seedy nightclub that sits at the water's edge next to a boat ramp. Most people that launch there know Liz like people at Cloverleaf know Sissy.

It is rumored that one can get hookers at Liz's, though the closest I've come to confirming this is what Dan and Ace told me and a few comments I've picked up sitting on the porch of other people's camps. And even then, I'm not sure how Liz gets away with it. It makes more sense to assume that many of the girls who hang out at Liz's become hookers as the opportunity arises.

It turned out that Ace had divorce on his mind and he wanted to tell me all of it. But with every third sentence simply "that crazy bitch," it was hard to piece the facts together. It was clear that she had cheated on him. It was also clear that Ace wanted to kill the lover and hurt the "crazy bitch." He would give me some details, pause to take a reflective swallow of beer, and then start in again.

We were about ten minutes into the story when I noticed that Dan was dry heaving at the ceiling. His head was still cocked over the back of the chair and eyes were closed. With each attack, his stomach puffed and his cheeks flared out. When Ace came to another pause in his story, I mentioned Dan's condition to him. Ace didn't look at his friend but waved his hand in the air, dismissing my concern.

"That crazy bitch," he continued. "I raised her. I built her car. That crazy bitch . . ."

"Ace, Dan is about to puke on himself. He might choke on it, drunk as he is."

"He's all right."

I started to stand. "It's not that I mind him pukin' on my floor, I just don't . . ."

Ace's arm swung over and knocked me back into the sitting position. "Siddown," he said.

I did. Ace stood up and staggered a few circles in the center of the room, apparently looking for something. Finally his eyes rested on my forty-gallon plastic trashcan. He pulled the garbage bag out of it and set it on the floor. Then he grabbed Dan's head by the hair and yanked it sideways and draped the can over it like a giant hat.

He sat down again. "That crazy bitch . . ."

I watched Dan's stomach, bloating and falling. Somewhere inside that trashcan, his cheeks were still flaring. I expected puke to come running down the inside of that can at any moment. But it turned out that Dan wasn't as helpless as he appeared. His hand left the armrest and began to dig around in his jeans pocket. It took a good thirty seconds, but he finally pulled out a folding knife and six inches of steel shot out of it with the flick of a finger. He then began to wave it wildly in front of him, as if to fend off whatever had mistreated him into the garbage can.

"Ace?"

". . . And she said, I'll be right back. And I said, take the keys, crazy bitch. You don't—"

"Ace?"

". . . my keys. My car. My—"

"Ace, Dan has got a knife and he's wavin' it about three inches from your knee."

"He's all right."

"I just wanted you to know about it."

As drunk as he was, I never would have believed he could move so fast. But it was instinctive. He didn't even look. Ace's hand flashed out and grabbed Dan's wrist in midair and shook the knife out. The knife clattered across the floor and Ace dropped Dan's wrist and stared down at his beer. Dan's arm flopped over the armrest and went limp. Not surprised. Defeated.

Over the next thirty minutes, Ace finished all the beer in his cooler. Then he instructed me to get my own cooler and he drank those, too. Eventually he ran out of story. He just kept repeating himself and he was having trouble keeping his neck from going limp. At one point, I thought he was about to pass out. It crossed my mind that he might wake up in my camp that morning and remember that I was also someone he wanted to kill. And I knew of no reason for me to have fallen off his list.

I was thinking of making a try for my bed when Ace suddenly stood and swatted the trashcan from Dan's head. Dan didn't move. His face was limp and he was at peace with whatever had haunted him.

"Get up, sumbitch!"

Dan didn't move. Ace grabbed a cooler handle with one hand and Dan's bicep with the other. He lifted his friend to his feet and began hauling his load toward the door. The last I saw of them that night, Ace was holding Dan by the back of the shirt as his friend hung pissing over my deck at a thirty-degree angle.

> This old boy used to show up at school back when we were kids. He always carried a paper grocery sack with his lunch in it. We never had much for lunch those days, so we was always wantin' to know what all he had in that sack. We figured it must be pretty good. Especially since he walked off to the top of the hill and ate it by himself every day.
>
> One day a few of us snuck up to the top of that hill and got up behind him. He opened the sack and pulled out two bricks and a hickory nut. He broke that hickory nut between those bricks and ate it while he looked out over the playground.

Chuckfee Revival

Steve talked me into holding a party. In a week we were having the first Chuckfee Revival, a live-band invitational.

"How much do you think it would cost to get Hank Williams Jr.?"

"I don't know. He's pretty washed up."

"Man, what if we got Hank! Nobody gets Hank for a private party. I'll bet we could get him for twenty thousand dollars."

"Where you gonna get twenty thousand dollars?"

"It might be worth it to use my savings. I'd have had Hank at the swamp camp."

"Crap."

We didn't get Hank, but we got the Leavin' Brothers. They'd simultaneously divorced their wives several years back, quit their jobs, and headed to Nashville in pursuit of a record deal. They'd simply left small-town Alabama for a better life. "Leavin'," they'd said.

After a long run of playing the country-music scene, they moved back home. No money. No wives. No job. No record deal. Now they came cheaper than Hank. It also didn't hurt that they were Steve's two older brothers. Invitations were printed and mailed. It was to be held in July.

About two weeks before the party, I began having nightmares about my camp sinking prematurely. I had a mental picture of every support under the camp, and it seemed impossible that it would hold the one hundred people we were inviting. Surely it would collapse.

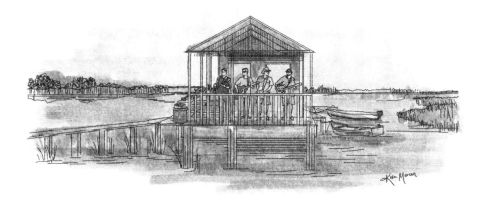

I spent the next weekend reinforcing the mudsills under the camp and nailing up extra floor joists. Then I called my insurance agent and took out an umbrella policy in case someone got hurt and they sued. As the date drew closer, I was no more at ease. How was the camp going to stay standing in mud the consistency of runny grits?

Meanwhile, Steve was organizing the band. The duties of obtaining beer kegs, whole hog, and snacks were divided between other camp members and their wives. T-shirts were being made. Shuttle boats coordinated. There was no stopping it. I was the only person who wasn't excited.

The party would start at noon on Saturday. I came up early the morning of and began inspecting the camp. The southeast piling looked like it could use some more mudsill, so I slopped some underneath and slapped down a board and wedged it into place. Still, I crawled back onto the deck and lay there thinking, "This is the end. All that work straight back to the mud. Nobody's ever put this many people on a swamp camp. It's going down and nobody cares. Nobody will help me rebuild. It's over."

It was late morning when the other camp members started arriving. By this time I'd calmed down a little. I'd brainwashed myself into the idea that if the camp was going down, then at least I would go down with it and the support of all my friends. I was kneeling in the water in front of the dock, soaking myself in the cool bay. The July heat fell over the swamp like hot breath and I wondered for the first time why we hadn't chosen a cooler date.

"You ready, man?" The approaching boat called out.

"I guess."

"Gonna be hot today."

"I know. I'm already hot."

"How many people you think are comin'?"

"I don't know. Depends on who all can get a boat ride. Then they have to find it."

"What are all those marked-up sticks jabbed in the mud?"

"So I can measure how much the camp sinks."

"Man, it's not gonna sink."

"How do you know?"

"You've been up here for two weeks haulin' stuff under there."

"I don't think it's enough."

"I'm tellin' you, it'll be fine. Let's unload this stuff."

The Leavin' Brothers and Steve arrived with the band equipment. They set up on the deck of the shop. The whole pig was arranged on the picnic table and the beer keg was positioned out front. The wives arranged hors d'oeuvres on the screen porch and stocked the bathroom with toilet paper. I piddled about the place, checking the generator, moving scrap lumber out of the way, trying to stay ahead of the trash that was starting to flutter about the camp.

That afternoon, the boats started moving into the bay like it was D-Day. "They found us," I said, full of dread. Actually, there were only about fifty guests, but that's a lot of boats and I'd never had more than ten people on my camp before. They tied up to the dock and helped their wives and girlfriends out and lugged their beer into the crowd. The Leavin' Brothers were pumping out country sounds and

I imagined that the swamp creatures were peering from the jungle, thoroughly confused.

People kept arriving all afternoon. Many of these guests I'd never seen before, swamp people lured from their boxes like moths to flame. Shirtless and sweating and drinking their own brands of beer. "Whose place is this?" they'd ask.

"It's Watt's."

"Show him to me."

"He's over there."

"You sellin' those T-shirts?"

"Yeah. Want one?"

"Hell yeah."

In between meeting swamp people and answering questions about how I'd built the camp way out there, I was almost too busy to drink a beer. It was obvious that the first annual Chuckfee Revival was a hit. Still nervous about the camp holding so many people, I continued to check the marks on my stakes to see if it was sinking. But the deck was still level with the top notch and my anxiety eased with each inspection.

Finally, as evening set in, most of the guests began to motor away. The whole hog was fly covered and stripped mostly to the spine. The beer keg floated in ice water and sacks of garbage lay stacked against the wall. The Leavin' Brothers had become too drunk to continue playing and they stumbled about with the rest of the remainders. The radio played AC/DC's "Back in Black" and a swamp couple slow-danced to it in their bathing suits.

The wives and girls were all gone. A group of ten members and friends were going to spend the night. With so many people coming and going out of the camp, it was impossible to keep the place air-conditioned. And once night fell, the insects began to pour in. We gathered into the steaming bug box and huddled around poker games or stood about wiping our foreheads with the backs of our arms.

"Close the damn door!" was yelled every few minutes.

The radio played out on the deserted deck, and frogs and other swamp creatures had come out of shock and resumed their normal activities. At some point, someone dragged what remained of the hog inside and flopped it onto the bar. A few people had thought to bring their own dinner and made trips back and forth to the grill.

That night was hell. There were only beds for six and that left the floor for the rest. But no one was going to sleep until the poker game was finished. Those who tried to sleep lay in bunks above the poker game, slowly basting in cigar and cigarette smoke, listening to the banter of man talk yelled out below. Moths and mosquitoes and flies hung in the hot air, and there was nothing to do but smother yourself away beneath a bedsheet and hope it would all end soon.

Just as the poker game ended, everyone who'd eaten the hog rushed outside and had violent spells of puking and diarrhea. They curled up on the porch, moaning in the fetal position.

Once the sick were settled outside and the rest of us in the bunks and on the floor, the air conditioner began to work. Beneath my thin sheet, my head throbbed from the coming hangover. I felt like I was lying in a battlefield with the wounded and dying all around me. And all daylight would bring was a cleanup of the poisons that had put us here. At least the air conditioning promised a small breath of relief, I thought.

Half an hour later, sunlight poured through the windows. People began moaning again. Rolling over and burying their faces from it. No one even had the energy to comment. I gave up and climbed down from my bunk and crossed the battlefield. I walked out onto the deck and made my way around the hog eaters.

Bill lay on the dock, cooling his face and scalp with a wet rag.

"Man," he mumbled. "We should have this party every year."

I checked the notches on my stakes. My camp had made it.

"I know," I said. "That was awesome."

Neighbors

*Me and this old boy was puttin' in at Cloverleaf one night. They had
    a juke joint back then where that old green buildin' is now. I was
    sittin' in the boat and that other fellow was backin' me down. I
    was about halfway in the water when I seen a gun barrel flash
    from the porch. Next thing I know, I hear the blast and there's
    lead shot hittin' the motor behind me.*

Somebody shot at you!

*Yeah. They shot again, too. I'd gotten down on the floor of the boat
    and I heard the pellets hit the side.*

They tryin' to kill you?

*I don't know. But I said to myself, they try that again and I'm gonna
    pick this thirty aught six up and give 'em some lead back.*

They shoot again?

*Yeah. I raised up with that deer rifle and squeezed off about five
    rounds at 'em.*

What'd they do?

They went back inside.

I'd been coming up to the swamp camp for five years. Cloverleaf
Landing was as familiar to me as my backyard. I lifted my hand and
waved to just about every person along my route up the Tensaw and
across the Raft and past Butch's camp into Chuckfee Bay. It was rare

that I didn't spend time over at Jack's or Dan's, depending on who happened to be up for the weekend.

Two things changed in my life that year. Foremost was the arrival of my first child, Adele, in November. My friends with children warned me that my delta days were numbered. As much as I loved my daughter and wanted to do what was right as a father, I carried a knot in my stomach when I thought of my creation in the swamp going to the mud and my writing time crowded out by family responsibilities.

I thought about my impending problem—not long, but hard. I realized that 80 percent of productivity is time management. So I quit my job to have more control over my time. I was going to be a freelance computer programmer. Control my time so that I could write more.

I soon realized that in addition to the financial stresses of being self-employed, you actually end up working more. But you do control your time. It was rare that I didn't arrange to take Friday afternoons off and stay up in the swamp until late Saturday morning. Swamping. Writing.

Once I was on this Friday schedule, I discovered that many other people coming to the delta are on similar schedules, arranging plans around what is convenient for their work and family. If they weren't up the entire week, Jack was mostly on a Saturday/Sunday schedule while Dan and Stacey were up for the entire weekend. So I began to spend more time over at Dan's camp on Friday nights.

> *Me and Carla was up late one night. I stepped outside to take a piss.*
> *I thought I heard somethin' and I looked off in the woods and*
> *seen the outline of a man out there.*
> *In the swamp?*
> *Just out there standin' in the mud.*
> *What in hell?*
> *He had pistols draped all over him like a Mexican bandit. After I*
> *squinted at him a minute I could tell it was Dan.*

What was he doin' out there?

That's what I asked him. I said, "Dan, what you doin' out there?" And he didn't answer me. So I said, "Dan, what the hell you doin' out there?" Still didn't answer me. I finally zipped up and walked back inside. I said, "Carla, Dan is out there with guns all strapped to him. He's just standin' out in the mud starin' at me and ain't sayin' nothin'. You call Stacey over at their camp and tell her he's out there." I walk back outside to keep an eye on him while Carla's callin' Stacey. He's still in the same place, starin' at me with those guns. We get to watchin' each other for a while then I hear lee-lee-lee-lee-lee. Lee-lee-lee-lee. Lee-lee-lee-lee. Finally he reaches down and pulls his cell phone from his belt and slams it to his ear and says, "Will you gimme a second!"

How'd your woodpile get messed up, Jack?

Dan come over last night and dove off the porch onto it.

He hurt himself?

We rode by his camp this mornin' and he was laid out on the front deck moanin'. We figured he was just drunk. We come by a few hours later and he was still there. Still moanin'.

What was wrong with him?

We asked him about it. He said he broke a rib.

Where do you work?

I'm in business for myself. I'm a computer programmer. How about yourself?

I work for the local 87.

Where do you work?

Depends on how clean my piss is.

Deltona 500

With the success of the first Chuckfee Revival, it was inevitable that people would pressure me to put it on again the following year. However, this time many of the camp members made it clear that they would not be spending the night.

Paul Stabler was elected to make the T-shirts again. The ones from the previous year were so popular that they'd become a sort of collector's item. It never ceased to amaze me how many strangers I ran into that recognized the shirt and had something to say about the party. Most of them had no idea that it was my camp, but the event had created a common bond across all strata of society.

The Leavin' Brothers couldn't make it for the second party, but we booked a solo guitar act that promised to be just as good. The party went off much like the first with the exception of a newly introduced main event: the Deltona 500.

The Deltona 500 was to settle the longtime argument of who could run Chicory Creek the fastest. The rules were as follows: only tiller-steered skiffs were allowed to race, and the first person to make the circular route from the camp, through Chicory, across Grand Bay, up Raft River, and back to the camp would be declared the winner.

As it turned out, only Coleman Briars and I qualified. Which was fitting, seeing as how we'd started the original argument. Coleman's boat had more horsepower, but I had more experience running the

creek. I reasoned that if I could beat him by a good stretch out of Chicory, he might not be able to overtake me on the river before I made it back to camp.

Riding bow with me was Charlie Yow, a college buddy and relatively new boy in the swamp. Steve took bow with Coleman. The start wasn't very official; I think I just gunned the motor and we were off. Coleman is very competitive, so I hope I don't get it wrong when I say that I believe I beat him to the mouth of Chicory. And if this was the case, then it was only because I surprised him at the start. Regardless, we were soon bottlenecked not far up the creek, like two wheelbarrows rammed side by side through the same slot. Both of our bow riders were leaning forward, yelling at the swamp like cheering would somehow pull them through. Soon our propellers were wound with weeds and ineffective. Our engines roared and smoked and spit mud water. Then I executed the move that I thought would ultimately win me the race. I slammed the motor into reverse, wound off my weeds, slammed it in gear again, and roared past Coleman. Once I had the creek to myself again, I kept the foot of my motor in the twelve-inch weedless slot running the center of Chicory. I wove it like a downhill skier, slowing only once when I had to stand and tilt my screaming engine over a submerged log. Coleman chewed away at the weeds for a while before he perfected the spinoff and lunged after me. He paused slightly to inspect the foot of his motor after slamming into the log but was soon closing in on me again like a mad bulldog.

As predicted, I beat him out of Chicory, but the lead was not comforting. "Hit the floor, Charlie!" I yelled as we raced into Grand Bay. "We need all we can get!"

Coleman's boat was leaping behind me like something insane. I saw him yell mutely at Steve and then Steve was down on the floor, too. At the other side of Grand Bay, we would come to another cutthrough that wasn't wide enough for both of us. I had to beat him to it. It was my last chance. If he got there first, he'd race on into the river and take me on the straightaway back to camp. "I gotta cut him off before we get to the pass," I yelled at Charlie. "Keep your fingers in the boat!"

I could almost reach out and touch the bow of Coleman's crazed vessel, riding my left wake. I cut hard in front of him and he smashed into my gunwales, knocking me straight again.

"What the hell!" Charlie yelled. I looked back at Coleman's boat and Steve was crouched down, wide-eyed and expressionless. Coleman's face was glowing like he was possessed. It was on.

"Stay down!"

"I am down. I just wanna stay in the damn—"

Wham! Coleman hit me on the port side. I quickly recovered and stared ahead at the pass. A hundred yards to go. I only had about a three-foot lead and he was right beside me. I cut it hard. Wham! My boat rose and fell, locking rails with the enemy. Both of us worked our tillers, trying to dislodge like fighting bucks with tangled antlers. We finally came apart and separated for moment before I turned into him again. Wham!

"Jesus!" Charlie yelled.

"Son of a bitch is about to lap us!"

The mouth of the pass is hard to find if you don't know exactly where to look. It's just a camouflaged opening in the swamp grass with only a small cypress tree for a landmark. Had Coleman been more familiar with the route, he might have been able to muscle me aside. But somehow he got off course and would have run up into the swamp had he not backed off. I shot ahead and plunged into the pass, weaving through it with the hammer down.

After all my effort and swamp tactics, he beat me on the straight-away. He arrived at the camp victorious. Which, truth be told, was fine with me. I'd gotten what I wanted out of it.

What do you do to a propeller to make it look like that?
I run it up in the delta a good bit. Get into some mud sometimes.
It's not just the prop, the whole engine looks like it was drug down the highway.
Well, that's why I brought it to your shop.

What happened to your boat, man?
I was racin' this friend of mine. We had to swap a little paint.

Boats on the Loose

I have a buddy that told me a story about an experience he and his father had in the delta. Their family has a houseboat that they keep south of the causeway. During duck season they will tie several Stauter skiffs to the back of it and motor up into the delta to create a mobile hunting lodge. One cold January weekend they arrived with their buddies and gear and anchored just south of Chuckfee Bay. They stayed up late the first night, grilling off the stern and drinking whiskey and carrying on like duck hunters will do. When they all finally settled into their bunks in the early morning hours, the wind was coming hard and icy out of the north and had the skiffs yanking at the stern.

Some hunters will dread the five o'clock wake-up call so much that they drift in and out of sleep, watching the clock to see when their comfort will end as much to make sure that they don't oversleep. Around four thirty that morning, one of the sleepless hunters got the feeling that something wasn't right. The steady yanking of the skiffs at the stern had ceased, yet the wind could still be heard outside. He rose and walked out onto the deck and looked around. The houseboat had washed downriver and they were beached in the shallows with the marsh grass waving around them. The skiffs were tangled about the boat like a splayed wind chime.

The hunter woke the others and their duck-hunting trip became a full day of getting the houseboat and the skiffs out of the mud. Later, upon inspection of the bow line, they saw that it had been cleanly cut with a knife.

Things like that happen in the delta. . . .

Sometimes delta experiences can cause a person to give up swamp life altogether. I think that's what happened to Steve, although I've never confirmed it. It was probably a good thing that he dropped his membership, although some of the best times I've had up there were with him. But we had both become fathers and had a tendency to get into a little too much mischief at times.

It was February. Steve, his neighbor Lance, and I were up for the night. We'd started drinking beer early that afternoon and by sunset the generator was purring in its little house and the porch lights were glowing to carry us into the night. Hank Williams Jr. played on the portable radio that stayed hidden beneath the sink. We grilled Cone-cuh sausage and steaks and toasted garlic bread.

The day had been clear and gusty and unusually warm for that time of year. But with the sun gone, the swamp grew still and the air cooled. Coons appeared from the marsh grass and stood on their hind legs to catch bits of leftover steak that we threw down to them. They disappeared to eat their scraps in privacy and reappeared to wait for more. There was no telling how many were out there. We called them swamp coons, and they were different from regular raccoons in that they were skinny and undernourished.

Not long after supper, we decided to go catch alligators. Lance was new to the delta and we'd built up the event to such heights that it was all he'd been talking about. Steve and I described the technique to him like we were old pros while he twitched and waited for us to put him on one.

Steve had a new boat that he was eager to use that night. It was an aluminum bass boat with cockpit seats and carpet and all of the gear. I considered it impractical and gave him a hard time about it, but Steve was always one to have the best gear and he ignored my comments.

As usual, the destination was Chicory Creek. We lugged the beer cooler into the boat, rigged up the Q-Beam, and set out with Lance riding the pedestal seat on the bow. Before we even reached the mouth of the creek, we put Lance on two small alligators and he hefted them into the air, studying them as if to show us he was not scared. Steve and I laughed and tipped our drinks.

We spent an hour idling the snaking turns of Chicory deep into the swamp, putting more beer in us, and laughing at worthless man talk. At one point we shut the engine off and drifted slowly, listening to the night sounds. We guzzled more beer, and the world became vague and painless.

On the way back to camp we stopped at the mouth of Chicory to let Lance grab one more alligator. I'd moved up to the pedestal seat at some point and had no intention of giving up my spot. Lance crawled in front of me and reached down and pulled the alligator from the water. About that time, Steve threw down on the accelerator and the boat lifted and plunged out into the bay. Lance lay across the bow, propped up on an elbow and holding the alligator out with the other arm. I felt the wind and the cool, humid air wiping across my face and wetting my hair. Steve turned the boat into the channel that ran back to camp. The bay was glass calm and any navigational hazards stood silhouetted against the horizon. The Q-Beam lay discarded and the boat's running lights were off. I knew the route well enough anyway and so did Steve. Or so he thought.

Just off the last point of land that we would have to round before reaching the camp, an old piling stuck up a few inches above the water. I saw it from my perch in the pedestal seat and my mind began to slowly contemplate it as we drew near. I thought, "Surely we won't hit that piling. Nobody ever really runs into those things."

But Steve raced on and the little peg drew closer. For good measure, I extended my arm and began curling and uncurling my finger to suggest altering our course north. "Surely he sees it," I thought. "He's seen that post a hundred times."

We hit the deadhead just left of center. I was catapulted into the air like a long jumper. When I hit the water, I was suddenly in a swirl of something like chocolate milk with no idea which way was up. All I could think was, "Where is the propeller?" Then I heard the "Ruuuuenhhhh" of the boat passing. I thrashed around a second more and felt my feet press into the soft mud of the bottom. I stood in three feet of water breathing hard and watched Steve and his boat make a slow turn to come back for me. Then I heard thrashing behind me. I turned to see Lance dog-paddling my way. He still had the alligator.

"What do I do!" he yelled.

"Stand up."

"What about the alligator?"

"Throw it."

I tell you about that old girl I found last week?

No.

I was out there on Raft River, headed to Cloverleaf. I seen this big shiny bass boat with a two-twenty-five Yamaha stacked up in the swamp. You could walk around it. . . . I didn't see nobody in it, so I just kept on. About two hours later I come back by and I seen that woman's hair hangin' over the side. I said, "Hell, it done knocked her out."

Was she dead?

I pulled up to the bank and set to hollerin' at her. That hair pulled in and she sat up. I asked her if anything was wrong. She said, "No, I'm just takin' a nap, waitin' for the tide to come in." I told her, "You gonna be waitin' a long time."

The Slough

Some nights we went deeper into the swamp than Chicory, or even the Trailer Park. There is one place that I have only been twice, and once I tell you about the first time, you may have concerns about my judgment.

The first time we went it was probably close to ten o'clock at night. Steve was driving my brother Reid and me in his boat. We had been winding through creeks, deep into the backwater, headed to a place that we only knew of from the big delta map in the camp. For reasons that will soon become clear, I am not going to name this place. We'll call it "the slough."

Our plan was to see the slough, turn off the motor, and drift and make man talk.

The dark wall of swamp eventually closed in around us, pressing the sides of our boat until we were forced to idle. It was early summer and the thrumming of the frogs overwhelmed even the boat engine. Occasionally the shadows of large birds passed above us as they broke the strip of sky overhead. We had been motoring a long time and each of us was lost in our own thoughts. I was feeling tired and wished we weren't so far from the camp.

The slough finally petered out into shallows where the swamp grass swayed against our disturbance. Steve shut off the engine and we began to drift. I sat beside him in a cockpit seat with the beer

cooler at my feet. My brother was on the bow. I didn't know what bothered me about the place at the time, but now I realize that I should have thought it strange that the frogs were suddenly quiet. There was no noise except the lapping of the boat against the still water. Then I started to take another sip of beer and noticed something in front of us that made the back of my neck tingle. Pulled up into the marsh were two boats.

"What in hell is that?" I heard my brother say.

"Boats," I replied.

"What are they doin' out here?"

"I don't know," I said, my mind racing through reasons for anyone to be out here at that time of night.

As we drifted closer, we saw that the boats were full of gear and just recently abandoned.

"Where are they?"

"Close," I said.

"Let's steal their crap," Steve said.

Even though I knew he was kidding, the moment Steve said those words, fear bolted up my spine.

"Shut the hell up, Steve. Whoever it is isn't far from here. They can probably hear everything we're sayin'."

"Where they gonna go?" he argued. "You can't walk around out there."

"I don't know. Just be cool."

We were all quiet for a few moments. I listened to the swamp but heard nothing.

"There's nobody out here," Steve said.

I didn't answer him. I took a sip of my beer and continued to listen. The boat drifted backward into a little stream off to our right, just enough so that the bow was still in the slough. Suddenly I saw a flashlight beam bouncing through the swamp to our right. Then I saw another. Then a gunshot fired from the same direction.

"What the—"

"Get us out of here!" I yelled.

Another gunshot came our way. "Get down on the floor, Reid!" I yelled.

Reid crawled onto the floor and I ducked low while Steve cranked the engine. He got it started and shoved the throttle forward. The boat surged and then hung. I realized instantly that the motor was lodged on something in the creek. Steve tried again with the same result.

"Shut it off!" I said as I leaped overboard.

He shut off the engine and I swam around to the rear of the boat until I felt the log we were hung over. Another gunshot came our way and I lifted the foot of the motor with adrenaline-pumped strength until it came up and over the log. Then I thrashed around to the side of the boat and began climbing in. "Go!" I said before I was even over the rail.

Steve started the engine again and hammered down on the throttle. The boat surged forward and out into the slough with me still climbing aboard. We kept it wide-open until we were miles from that place.

We talked about that night for months afterward, guessing at what those people might have been doing. Either they heard Steve talking about stealing their gear and took it seriously, or they were up to something they didn't want us to know about. I decided that it was a little of both.

The story of us getting shot at became such a camp staple that it was inevitable someone would eventually convince us to show them where it happened. And by my reasoning, if people had fired on us for threatening to steal their gear, then we had only to not make that threat again. If they were doing something illegal out there, then surely they would have gotten spooked at us discovering them and moved on. It seemed highly unlikely that we would encounter those same people in the slough again.

The night we returned, we saw boats pulled up into the marsh in the same place. This time we did not stay but turned back quickly. I've not been back since.

The Boat Slip

On the northwest corner of Sissy's property lay the ruins of two rows of boat slips. The north row was completely stripped of its roof. The south row still had some rusty sections of tin that lifted and fell with the river wind. The access dock to both had long since rotted and been swept away by high water. To me, those boat slips represented not only another profit center for Sissy but also the ideal accessory for my swamp writing efforts.

I approached Sissy about fixing them up and she told me that she'd already been thinking about it. I asked if I could rent a slip from her when it was done and she agreed.

Repairs and renovations don't happen fast at Cloverleaf. For two years I asked Sissy every couple of months how much longer it would be. The answer was always the same: "Next month."

Finally I offered to make the repairs myself in exchange for a few months of free rent and an ongoing lease on the boat slip. Sissy agreed. Carson pointed to the coffee can full of rainwater next to the hackberry tree where I would find some framing nails. Then he walked over and kicked at a pile of rusted sheet tin.

"I can get new tin and some roofing nails," I offered.

"Hell, it'll hold," Carson responded.

My cousin Connor was with me, and the two of us spent the better part of the morning banging around on top of the old structure and placing the sheets of tin where they would cover my stall. The plank walk that got us out there was close to something you'd find in a Dr. Seuss book, but it held underfoot and Sissy promised that they would have it more stable in a month.

I had a boat slip. And I felt like I'd just one-upped every other swamp camper in the territory. I even built a second plank walk that ran along the side of my boat so that loading and unloading gear was easier. It was during this construction that I first learned of Carson's tolerance for electricity.

I needed power for the circular saw I was using to trim the decking for my plank walk. Carson told me that I would find a plug around the back of the bait shop.

"Just reach in that window back there and you'll feel it," he told me.

I took my extension cord and trudged through the marsh between the boat slips and the bait shop. When I got to the window, I stuck my hand into the dark hole and felt around. I leaped backward when my fingers probed an open socket. "Crap!" I said to myself. I started for the bait shop to get a second opinion from Carson but then thought better of it and shook my head. I took the end of the cord again and fed it into the hole. I scraped the prongs around the socket until I felt a match and shoved it home. The electric shock that coursed through me made me clench my teeth. I leaped back with the plug and shouted "Crap!"

Carson was fixing his tractor.

"Carson, I tried to plug that cord in and it shocked the hell out of me."

"It'll hit you sometimes."

"Well, it hit me good."

Carson dropped his wrench and I followed him back to the bait shop. He picked up the plug from the ground, stuck his hand in the hole with it, twitched his cheek, and withdrew.

"There you go," he said.

Mayhall

One evening Jack brought his older brother Mayhall to my camp. Mayhall is a giant. His handshake wraps your hand like you were a baby. The most striking of his features are a full head of snow-white hair and perfect teeth that shine from a workingman's face. Once the serene vision of Mayhall has settled on you, his laugh causes you to take a step back. It comes out like a hyperventilating truck.

Mayhall had been an Alaskan crab fisherman before moving back to Alabama. His southern accent has been eroded enough by his travels to make him sound smarter than the rest of us. And I was soon to find out that he was just as hospitable and had just as many entertaining stories as his brother.

Like Jack, Mayhall had grown up fishing and hunting the delta. He had already arranged for a lease just down from Jack's camp and the talk was heavy with plans for his new camp. His wife, Suzy, was all for the idea and seemed to be just as excited as Mayhall.

> There was this one place we'd come through on the way in from crab fishin'. We passed about a mile away from this big cliff about two hundred feet high. There were walruses stacked from the water to the top of that cliff. Thousands of 'em. Big old sons of bitches. This fellow gets up on the deck one day with a deer rifle and shoots a few rounds from the hip at that wall. We all stood around

watchin', but nothin' happened. About a half a minute later, we
saw those walruses start fallin' off the cliff.
You go get their tusks?
Naw, we had to get those crabs in.

Mayhall was retired from his days of fishing in Alaska. He had moved
back to Baldwin County and worked two weeks on, two weeks off, as
a boat captain on vessels that supplied the offshore drilling operations
in the Gulf. This schedule allowed him to complete his swamp camp
faster than any I'd witnessed. I saw the pilings set one weekend and
the next I saw walls and a roof. He was immediately established and
positioned to become another good friend of mine.

Besides being good company, Mayhall also taught me about smoked
mullet. When he first described it to me, I imagined what most people
would: a fillet of mullet smoked to something like kippered salmon. I
was wrong. The mullet may have been smoked, but I was to first experience it in the form of a giant glob of sandwich spread—mayonnaise
and ground mullet kneaded in a salad bowl. Having never been a fan
of mayonnaise, I was a bit standoffish when it was placed before me.
But I was a polite house guest and forced down a share.

Outside of tuna fish, I had only heard of serving fish in this way
one other time. I was fishing a small slough in the north delta when
I slipped up on two men fishing with giant fifteen-foot cane poles. I
call these poles blackfishing poles because until then I had only seen
them used to catch a large, perch-like fish in the ship channel called
a blackfish. The men had walked down to this slough through the
swamp on a trail historic to their community and set themselves upon
five-gallon buckets. They would swing their long poles out to place
their corks over the deepest part of that black water. Within seconds
they would drag a flopping grinnel onto the bank, unhook it, and toss
it onto a pile of many others beside them. A grinnel is a bony, prehistoric, bottom-feeding species sometimes called a bowfin outside of

the south. It is typically thought of as a trash fish, although I must admit I've tasted many fish that do not deserve that name. The blackfish being one of them. But I'd never known anyone to pursue grinnel.

"What you gonna do with all those?"

"Eat 'em," one of the men replied casually.

"How do you cook a grinnel?"

"Boil it. Grind it up and spread it on toast."

I assumed that the five-gallon buckets would be turned over and used to carry their catch back with them once they'd caught what they needed. Regardless of what I thought about ground grinnel on toast, when I think about simple and pleasant, I'm always reminded of those two sitting on the buckets under the shade of giant cypress trees swinging fish out of that slough.

Those mullet are pretty small.

Gonna can 'em.

How do you do that?

Put 'em in a mason jar with a jalapeño. Boil it. Make you forget about all that other stuff.

Where'd you get all those spoonbills nailed on your wall?

Caught 'em.

Those things good to eat?

They'll eat. Cut 'em in little slivers. I don't like 'em all chunked up.

Taste that.

What is it?

Taste it.

Looks like rotten Spam.

It ain't. Put it in your mouth.

. . . Damn. Pretty good.

Hogshead cheese. Buddy of mine made it.

Delta Heckler

A friend of Reid's said he had a pontoon boat in Alexander City, Alabama, that he didn't want. It had sunk in Lake Martin and never been used since. All he required of the transaction was someone to haul it away.

Reid purchased a used boat trailer and started north. He knew about engines and bodywork, and we were confident he could restore it to functional shape, regardless of its condition. On my end, I secured a second boat slip from Sissy and fantasized about the amount of lumber I was going to be able to barge up on our new man tool.

Once Reid restored the engine and patched the pontoons, we stripped it of everything except the railings and built a steering console and storage box out of treated plywood. Then we accessorized it with a CD player, a utility plug for a Q-Beam, and a PA system. Finally, we purchased some plastic lawn chairs and scattered them about the deck. My father saw it and described it as the "most God-awful, red-neck thing he'd ever seen." Reid and I described it as perfect. After testing and approving the PA system, we named it the Delta Heckler.

The pontoon boat created a whole new dimension of entertainment. Although sluggish and unwieldy, it came at a time in our lives when we didn't have many responsibilities and a slow ride on a party barge was ideal. We would tie the jon boats to the back and load gear and friends onto the deck and set out for the swamp camp.

One problem with the Heckler was its ability to fool you into believing it could drive itself: it was so sluggish and turned so slowly. Once underway, it was not uncommon for the driver to walk to the front of the boat and join the rest of the passengers. It usually became unclear whose responsibility it was to adjust the course as the river bend came closer. And sometimes it was fun to purposely forget. The first time the boat ran aground at full-bore, people were thrown to the deck and out into the swamp, but no one was hurt. And once we pushed our vessel back into the river, we saw that it still floated. From then on, violent beaching of the Heckler joined the ranks of alligator catching for entertainment.

As an additional bonus, the Heckler was also ideal at running Chicory Creek. Instead of taking the turns like a downhill skier, one could drive the pontoon boat straight ahead, bouncing up onto one pontoon across the juts of land. After several trial runs, we perfected the technique by having passengers rush to the on-water side of the boat just before the opposite side ran aground. This lifted the on-ground side just enough to keep the boat moving at top speed.

This was the beginning of the end for the Heckler. It wasn't long before the pontoons began leaking again, this time from wearing the aluminum thin on the bottom. It began sinking in the boat slip from slow leaks. Then we hauled it out and took it to a shade tree welder that did even more damage. Finally we slapped pancake-sized patches of J-B Weld on the bottom and that became the solution of choice when new leaks occurred.

"Is the Heckler floatin' right now?" was the first question asked when planning excursions to the swamp camp. And it was probably better if the answer was no. The pontoons had been patched so many times that just because it still floated in the stall didn't mean it wouldn't start leaking when loaded with gear and passengers.

I was in my bunk one morning when an early riser woke me. "The pontoon boat sank last night," he said.

"How bad?"

"One side of it is totally submerged."

I closed my eyes again and rolled over. "It's all right, then."

Later that morning Reid and I loaded everyone aboard and had them stand toward the front left to try and level the boat. This helped enough to keep the fuel cans from floating around in the back. Then we cranked the engine and began our journey back to Cloverleaf.

Mile two, the passengers were huddled and perched on the tip of the good pontoon like men with alligators snapping at them. Water flowed over my feet at the steering console and I was beginning to lose my nerve. By the time we saw Cloverleaf, the back of the engine was underwater and its white exhaust bubbled behind us. If we slowed, we were going down. I aimed for the cement boat ramp and kept the throttle down.

The sunken side of the boat was riding so low that we ran aground about five feet before the ramp. My passengers leaped off and the bow rose into the air like something from the Titanic so that I had to hold onto the steering wheel to keep from falling backward.

Carson stood on the hill next to his diesel truck, eyeing the situation like he'd been waiting for such a project for two days. "Y'all need some help?" he hollered at us.

"Think you can pull it up the ramp so we can drain this water?"

"Got-damn right I can!"

Carson plunged into his truck bed. He reappeared with a tow strap and backed his truck down the ramp. We connected the Heckler to the tow strap and tied the other end to his trailer ball. "Go!"

It was one of the most awful sounds I'd ever heard—the Heckler getting lynched up the cement. I knew that even when we got the water drained from the pontoon, there might be little life left in our old friend. Then I looked back at the engine. It was completely submerged. The heart of the thing drowned.

It took close to an hour for the pontoon to drain. We had a good-sized crowd gathered around us, both to gape at the ruin and to wait until we were out of the way so they could get their own boat in the river. Finally we got it to float enough so that we could get the trailer under and pull it up the ramp.

While the backed-up patrons began launching their boats, Reid and I surveyed the damage. There was a large hole in the front of the pontoon from dragging it over the cement. The support frame was bent along the front where we had been winching it onto the trailer like a wet mattress. But these things could be fixed with J-B Weld and a hammer. It was really the engine we were worried about.

Reid dismantled and began to clean and dry the carburetor. I kept circling the boat, looking for more pontoon damage. I heard a couple of beers pop behind me.

After ten minutes, Reid put the carburetor back together and stood, wiping his hands on his shirt. "Let's see if it'll crank," he said, turning the key. The flywheel came to life and spun like it had a hot battery. Reid kept the pressure on, but the engine wouldn't fire.

"Think the spark plugs are good enough?" I asked.

"They were this mornin'."

"Maybe they got water in 'em or somethin'."

"It wouldn't hurt to clean 'em."

"Hold on," Carson said, setting his beer down. He walked over to the motor and pulled one of the two spark plug cables loose. He grabbed the end of the connected plug with his hand. "Hit it," he said.

"You crazy, Carson?"

"Hit it," he said again.

I looked at Reid. "He said hit it, Reid."

Reid shrugged and turned the key. Carson's face didn't even twitch. I'd mistakenly touched a live spark plug on a lawnmower before and it had nearly knocked me down. My hand had ached and throbbed for close to an hour afterward. I couldn't believe what I was seeing. Reid let off the key.

"That'ns good," Carson said. He reconnected the loose wire and pulled the other one loose and grabbed the second plug. "Hit it," he said again.

"Crap," I said. "Hit it again, Reid."

Reid laughed and twisted the key. Carson stared away at the ground like he was reading the health of the electrical pulse through his fingers. He finally let go. "Both of them got-damn plugs is good."

We finally got the motor started with the help of ether sprayed into the carburetor. I shook hands with the camp members that had stayed for the show, hooked up the Heckler, and dragged it home.

After patching the pontoons, we tried keeping it in the stall again, but it was never the same. Like an old boxer that just didn't have it in him anymore. I started getting more calls at work than usual about the Heckler sinking, and it just became too much of a hassle to deal with. Now it sits in my yard under the mulberry tree, stained purple with berry juice. I'm pretty sure my wife thinks about it even more than I do these days.

Camp Names

What's the name of your camp?
Well, we've got a sign that says the Boar's Nest, but we've always just
*   called it the Swamp Camp.*
I thought it was the Double-Barrel.
We were gonna call it that for a while, but it just didn't take.
Why don't you just name it the Swamp Camp.
I don't know. I guess being a swamp writer and all, I feel like I
*   should have a better name.*
Nobody else calls theirs the Swamp Camp.
Maybe I will.

I did finally decide to call it the Swamp Camp. It made sense. It named itself, which I suppose should be the most legitimate way to get a name. Camp names are an important part of the delta.

Whiskey Breath

Stud Duck

Soggy Bottom

Goggle Eye

Roll Tide

Raft River Hilton

Hard-Knock Café

Kittyhawk

Delta Shelta

AcunaMatada

Isle Mirada

Delta Dream

Camp Hog

Stagger Inn

Runamuck

Stumpknocker

Bull Frog

Red

Mr. Corley died about five years into my lease. The land went to his children, some of whom lived out of town. Rumors began circulating that the children wanted to sell the land and that our leases wouldn't hold up in court. Complications of every description began to surface until those of us on the south bank of Chuckfee Bay were in a panic. I went to Jack for advice.

"I guess they gonna do what they gonna do," he said.

"What have you heard?"

"They said Mayhall's lease wadn't any good. Said he signed it after Corley was dead."

"What's he say about that?"

"Says to hell with it."

"What about *our* leases?"

"They said you've got a huntin' lodge goin' on over there."

"Huntin' lodge!"

"Said it's against the rules."

"What? What rules? I don't have a huntin' lodge! I've never made a cent off that place."

"I heard they was gonna go up on the rent by five hundred dollars."

"That's no big deal. It's worth it to me."

"I can't afford that."

I suddenly felt bad for saying it. "Well, who do we send our rent check to? Who do I talk to about this huntin' lodge crap?"

"They got some big lawyer now from Bay Minette. Some guy named Red Wilkins."

"Red Wilkins?"

"Yeah. You heard of him?"

"Hell, Jack, we're set. Mr. Red's my next-door neighbor where I grew up."

Red played football for Bear Bryant in the early 1960s. He is a hulking man of six feet six inches, two hundred fifty pounds with red hair and a slow, booming, southern drawl. He is the most intimidating figure I have ever met and an entire book could be written about him alone. I often wonder what it would be like to see Red and Mayhall Johnson go to blows.

I called Mr. Red about the camp situation. He addresses my brothers and me with "bo" following our name. I've always assumed it was short for "boy."

"Wattbo, how you been?"

"Fine, Mr. Red."

"How's your daddy?"

"He's fine."

"How's Reidbo?"

Mr. Red's always been overly fond of my brother Reid. "He's fine, too."

"That's good. What can I do for you?"

"I heard you were handling the Corley estate. You know Reid and I have a camp up there."

"Yeah, we're tryin' to get it worked out. I hear they got some problems with people up there."

"They think I have a huntin' lodge."

"They didn't say anything to me about that."

"That's good. I'm not doin' anything wrong up there."

"You'll be all right. Tell me what you know about all that mess."

"Well, they're some rough people up there. They hear their leases might not get renewed and their rent's gonna go up. They're pretty riled about it."

"Who we gotta run outta there?"

"Run out?"

"Ain't gonna have no troublemakers up there."

"Well, I don't wanna mention any names. They'll burn your camp down up there."

"Who will?"

"Lots of those folks."

There was a pause on his end of the line. "We'll see about that," he finally said.

"You think I'll be able to keep my lease?"

"You'll be all right. Just send me your rent check. Ain't gonna be no burnin'."

I was always concerned about being burned out. When I was a boy someone burned my father's hunting camp to the ground. I knew firsthand how quick so much hard work and good times could be taken from me.

And I had reason to be concerned. The Hargett camp, just down from me, had burned a few weeks before. Reid had gone up early one morning and been the first to discover it smoldering in the morning fog, nothing left but a pile of ashes and a wire dog kennel.

I asked Jack about it.

"Some say electrical. Some say they got burned."

"Who'd burn 'em?"

"Supposedly those boys got into it with somebody. I've heard some names."

"Nobody around here?"

"Naw, I don't think anybody around here."

It seems that every swamp person but me has a sheriff of some re-
lation that they can get involved in these issues. The Hargetts were no
exception. They had an investigation going on, picking through the
ashes and such. And I'd hate to be the fellow they eventually point the
finger at. Those Hargetts are some big boys. I've passed by a couple of
times since while they were kicking about in the ruins. I made sure
to wave.

Horace

I sent my check to Mr. Red, and over the next few months the rumors died out. Everybody sat back down and picked up their cane poles again. All except for Mayhall. Even though he'd just finished his new camp, he found a deal on another one up in Oak Bayou about a quarter-mile away and bought it. It was his backup plan.

"What you gonna do with that camp you just built, Mayhall?"

"Gonna let Horace and my son use it."

Horace was one of Mayhall and Suzy's friends I had met a few times. They had referred to him as their son once or twice, which I later found out wasn't true. They corrected me and said that he was not technically their son but thought of as such. Which still confuses me. I have yet to get a straight answer as to who exactly Horace is and where he comes from and the nature of his relationship with Mayhall and Suzy. Once Horace told me that he was working in Alaska. The next time I met him, he was working in Washington. Then he was living somewhere in Baldwin County. Then down visiting from Washington again. Don't get me wrong, I like Horace and it has never crossed my mind that he's a liar. Every time I see him, he is always eager to help me fix my generator or figure out my constant electrical issues. I'm just surprised that I have never gotten to the bottom of his existence in the delta.

But there were many swamp people I still hadn't figured out. For instance, there is one fellow I've seen pass in front of my camp for years. It is usually late in the afternoon. I wave and sometimes he waves back. I think, "Surely I'll run into that guy at someone's camp one day and find out who he is." But I never do. He passes by and disappears around the bend and won't come back by until the next day. I guess he stays back there somewhere—at one of only about six camps that I know. Not real sociable.

There's this other fellow about my age, Hodgson, who is so henpecked that he doesn't make it up much. When he does, you can tell he's having a miserable time just thinking about the hell he's going to catch when he goes home. And as if that's not enough, all the swamp people pick on the poor guy so much that I don't understand why he doesn't give up swamp life altogether. But he won't. He loves it too much.

He's actually got his own camp, if you can call it that. It's the tiniest, most lonesome-looking thing I've ever seen. Nothing more than a six-by-eight lawnmower shed sitting on some oil drums and tucked into this little cove where no one would ever go. I don't see how he even stretches out to sleep in the thing, much less has company over. I like to ask him about it, just to see if maybe he'll admit one day that he wants something a little bigger. But he loves to talk about it and gives no indication that he's any less proud of his place than I am of mine.

But I think Hodgson gets lonely. He seems to prefer staying at someone else's camp and having people to talk to when he can. They pick on him and joke about towing his little houseboat off in the night and leaving it where he can't find it. He just takes it all and sleeps on their floor and goes home in the morning.

Hodgson came by my camp one afternoon and tied up to the dock. He sat in his boat for a while, drinking beer, watching me hammering something together. It didn't take long to figure out he wanted me to invite him to stay over. I was planning to spend the night writing alone, but it's not too hard for me to put company ahead of writing when the sun starts setting out there.

We'd made a sort of connection a few months before, when Hodgson had asked me about all the books in my camp. I would guess that not many, if any, swamp people keep a bookcase of books in their camp. And I don't know how often Hodgson just tells people what they want to hear, but he said he liked to read. I gave him a Larry Brown book that I thought he'd like and he remembered me for it.

Bottle Creek

In 1200 AD the Pensacola Indians built a ceremonial center in the upper delta. The ruins of this complex are now known as the Bottle Creek Mounds. Most similar archaeological sites were discovered and looted long before they were appreciated for their cultural significance. Because of its remote location, Bottle Creek wasn't even mapped until the late 1800s. Its eighteen mounds that served as platforms for houses and temples make it the largest Mississippian site on the north-central Gulf Coast. The largest of these mounds stands nearly fifty feet high.

The first time I went in search of Bottle Creek I took my father-in-law, Mike, and my six-year-old son, Albert. I hadn't spent much time in that part of the delta so I came prepared with a map and word-of-mouth advice from several locals. Accordingly we launched in the late afternoon at Upper Bryants Landing just north of Stockton. From there we ran down the Tensaw and motored miles through a creek so narrow and shallow that I considered turning back several times. Eventually we emerged in Bottle Creek not far from the mounds.

Finding Bottle Creek took us much longer than I'd planned for. And even when we arrived it took us a while to locate the sandy foot trail leading up the creek bank and back into the palmetto bottom. There were no signs, no people, no trash. Just a small creek with still, black water in the absolute middle of nowhere. The place is very quiet

except for the thrum of cicadas and the occasional fish popping at a surface bug.

The sun was already cooling below the treetops and I was feeling anxious. It was obvious that we'd have to make the return journey after nightfall, a trip I wasn't looking forward to. Even more worrisome was the idea of being on foot deep in the swamp without a flashlight. Especially as host to my son and my father-in-law.

We tied my skiff to a tree branch and set out under a shroud of tall cypress trees and hackberry. We hurried up the footpath, rasping through the palmetto, hopping mud holes and small creeks. At that point I really just wanted to check the place off my list and get out of there as fast as I could. I certainly didn't expect what I was about to find.

After about a half mile we began to see the mounds standing eerily out of the gloom. My anxiety melted away and I slowed my pace, at once humbled and reverent. I immediately understood what the pioneers felt when stumbling across an Indian burial ground. I'm sure the pending darkness added to my mood, but even so, the place was downright spooky and unnerving.

The footpath snaked through the ruins until it finally led us to the largest mound, rising nearly fifty feet and disappearing into the trees. We climbed it and stood at the top, our heads literally in swamp canopy. I would have liked to have spent more time there, but my son complained that the mosquitoes were biting and I was reminded of our predicament. I put him on my shoulders and we all started back as night fell around us.

By the time we got back to the boat, night had fallen. There was no cell phone coverage and I didn't want to risk running out of gas in the narrow, isolated creek we'd fought through to get there. I got Albert in his flotation vest and settled. Then I started thinking fast.

"Hold the flashlight," I told Mike. "I think I know a shorter way back."

Mike held the light while I studied the map for a cut I'd noticed earlier. I soon found it, what looked like an old logging ditch north of us. I pointed and he saw it, too, and that was good enough to plan on but not enough to ease the knot in my gut.

We ran a mile up the Tensaw, waving the spotlight across the riverbank. I felt like a horse kicked me in the stomach when we saw channel markers in the Mobile River. The cut wasn't there.

"We're gonna have to turn around," I said.

If Mike was worried, he didn't show it. He's always carried an optimistic outlook, but I thought this might just tip him. So I didn't mention that turning around sentenced us to running out of gas somewhere in the vast swamp.

"I'm tired, Daddy," Albert said.

I had a sleeping bag in my dry box and I got it out for him. "Just lie down on the floor and go to sleep," I said, calmly.

I turned the boat around and started back. I decided if we were going to run out of gas it would be best to take a longer, more established route so there was at least a chance we'd run into people.

After a while I saw Albert was asleep and I slowed the boat. It was time to come clean to my father-in-law just how much I'd screwed up.

"We're not going to make it," I told him. "We're almost out of gas. I need to find a camp in case we have to spend the night."

"Is there somebody we can call?"

I took a deep breath. "I don't have a signal. Maybe I will when we get closer."

I didn't mention the low-battery warning blinking on my phone. I'm glad it was too dark to see his face. I felt like a fool.

I drove with one hand on the tank, tilting it, judging the weight. Even when I was sure it could be nothing but fumes, I kept on. Finally I saw an abandoned camp and shut off the motor and drifted before it. The sound of frogs and cicadas and emptiness pressed into us over the black water. I got my phone out and stood on the bow and held it over my head. One bar. I called my wife.

"I don't have time to explain. We're out of gas. Call Archie and tell him to track down David and give him my number."

"Where are you?"

"Somewhere off the Tensaw. Albert and your dad are okay. My phone's about to die."

There was only one person I knew who could find us. David Steele of the White Car fame. And my friend Archie could find *him*. In the upper delta David was the closest thing to a swamp rat I knew. The last time I'd seen him was ten years before and we'd chatted about a family trip he was taking to Disney World.

In five minutes my phone rang. I answered it. There was no small talk.

"Hey, bud. What do you see?"

My low-battery alarm bleeped. I had ten seconds.

"We just made a left turn out of a river about fifty yards across into a wide area. There's an old camp on my right."

"Got a big stump stickin' out of the water twenty feet in front of you on the left?"

I squinted. "Yeah. I see it."

"Orange bream cork hangin' on it?"

I saw a faint orange speck. "Yeah?"

"Stand by."

My phone bleeped again and went black.

An hour later I heard a boat moaning toward us through the night. It seemed we listened to it approaching forever. The only man-made noise on earth. Then I saw a vaguely familiar psychedelic neon beer mug floating through the air over a vessel that was otherwise dark. The mug passed, purple and orange and blinking not thirty feet from our faces, and kept on into the night. Boat waves rocked us gently.

I looked at Mike. Back at the disappearing mug.

Slowly the boat made a wide circle and I heard David and Archie laughing over the still water. And I recalled seeing a similar mug for sale at the Rainforest Café at Disney World.

With good friends ten years always seems like yesterday.

No-Name

The largest living alligator that I know of in the delta makes his territory almost exactly halfway between Cloverleaf and my camp. There is a high piece of ground along the riverbank where he suns himself in flattened swamp grass. I call him No-Name.

I was coming up by myself one day in the middle of the week. The river was dead calm and no one was about. As always, I looked for the alligator after I rounded the bend in Raft. But he was not there that day and I decided to take the opportunity to look over his sunning area.

When I nudged my jon boat against the riverbank, it seemed that even the birds were silent. Stepping up into the matted grass brought to mind a medieval knight creeping into a dragon's lair. I doubted that many human feet had ever been where I was going.

As I stood there in the silence, the first thing I noticed was a shallow stream running just behind the matted grass. In the streambed were what looked to be hog bones, dyed yellow from the mud like smokers' teeth. I scanned the ground around me and saw bird feathers and the rib cages of smaller animals scattered about. A chill passed up my spine and raised my neck hairs. I turned and left as quietly as I'd come.

Sometimes, especially when I have passengers, I will steer my boat directly toward the alligator without reducing speed. This is en route

to or from the camp and we will have been underway for almost ten minutes. A long enough time for my crew to be calm and content and to trust my judgment concerning the river course. And No-Name cannot be easily seen from the low jon boat. Only the rough, black outline of his back appears through the strain of swamp grass.

When the boat begins to get unusually close to the riverbank, my passengers will act on instinct and turn to check my attentiveness. I stare ahead at the riverbank. They are then satisfied that I'm alert and also curious about what I'm searching for.

About ten feet from the bank, No-Name will leap out into the river. He is not after us but eager to get to safety underwater. But this leap appears to be directed at the people riding up front. No-Name's entry into the water is a violent thrashing of spray and black fury. As I turn the boat to miss him, my crew is piling toward me, expletives flying.

> *You ever seen that big alligator on Raft?*
> *Which one?*
> *That one that sits in the grass about halfway between the bend and
>   Crab.*
> *Hell yeah, I seen it! I shot that sumbitch.*

I thought back to the last time I'd seen No-Name. It had been a couple of months. I was sorry that the man had shot it, but I didn't say it to his face. But the next week I saw No-Name again. Whichever sumbitch he'd shot wasn't the same. And he's still lying there waiting to entertain my guests.

Random Proud

It may have been the worst-looking vessel I'd ever seen, tied to a plank walk he'd built out into the river at Cloverleaf. A blue-hulled houseboat about forty feet long. The fellow working on it advertised himself with a paint-specked jam box blaring Night Ranger songs. I'd heard the radio and seen him out there every day I'd come up in the last month.

"Lookin' good," I called out to him.

He walked away from the radio and toward me. The plank walk shook and I studied the water below and did a quick reassessment of the construction under my feet. Once he reached me, he turned again and took in his creation. "Yeah," he said. "Gettin' there."

"Does it run?"

"Hell yeah. Got two diesels."

"Gonna live on it?"

"If my old woman don't get off my back. I've thought about it."

I never cease to be amazed at the simple things that make swamp people proud. One afternoon I drove up to the landing to find Carson sitting on the tailgate of a truck with three older men. They were drinking beer with three large coolers at their feet. As I got out of my truck and approached them, I detected something mischievous in their silence and expressions.

"Y'all knockin' 'em back, Carson?"

"We been drinkin' all day," one of the other men said.

"Yep. All day and ain't pulled one fish in the boat," Carson remarked.

"Well," I said, "at least you had a good time."

There was a pause while the three looked at each other and smiled.

"Check out what they caught," Carson finally said. He reached down and lifted the lid to one of the coolers. It was stacked full with large crabs.

"Damn," I said. "Y'all got crab traps out there?"

"Hell no!" Carson said. "They caught ever got-damn one of these on a hand line."

I was familiar with hand lines. We'd used them growing up on the bay. The basic idea is to take a piece of string and tie something heavy on the end to weight it. Then you attach a chicken neck or some other piece of tough meat near the weight and suspend it in the water. A crab will start feeding on the bait and hang on even when you pull the string up close enough to scoop the crab into a net. Sometimes if there are a lot of crabs in the area, you can scoop two or even three at a time. It's great entertainment for kids but not the most efficient means for catching crabs.

"You lined all these!"

"Three coolers' full," one of the men said proudly.

"How'd you have time to drink?"

"We found most of 'em about an hour ago."

How long you think this'll take? Should I come back later?

You sit right there and you'll see it done in about ten minutes. You're lucky you got me, though.

You pretty fast at puttin' on trailer hitches?

Number eleven in the country.

They have contests for trailer hitch installations?

Company tracks it. U-Haul sent us a report. Said I was number eleven.

I drank two and a half cases of beer today.

How in hell do you drink that much? You're skinnier than I am.

I told that son of a bitch I'd match him drink for drink until he passed out, then I'd drink that much again and haul him home.

Where is he?

In there passed out.

What's up, dude?

Throw me your bow line. Glad you could make it. We got a keg, barbecue pig, and somebody's gonna start playin' guitar in a little while.

I brought some corn. Silva Queen.

Bring it on.

Lemme see if I can find it. I think it rolled under the boat seat.

Best Friends

Typically I will use the public launch about a mile down the road when I am setting out from the causeway. One day I decided to try Liz's for a change of scenery. After a long day of piddling at the camp, I returned just after dark and went inside to pay my three-dollar launch fee. The club was in fine form with smoke billowing out of the door and a jukebox playing rock and roll music. I recognized a few people I might have known well enough to nod at, but otherwise, I was in unfamiliar territory. By the time I'd worked my way to the bar to pay Liz, I felt like people were watching me.

Liz took a five from me and I waited while she made change. I happened to glance down the bar and see Ace a few stools away staring at his drink. An instant panic coursed up my spine. I had not seen him since the night he and Crazy Dan had paid me a visit. I'd thought about that night many times since and I'd never figured out why a person so determined to kill me at one time would have such a change of heart. I'd concluded that he'd been so drunk that night he'd forgotten who I was. Since then, perhaps he'd remembered? Maybe he'd subtracted that entire episode of the late-night visit and was still left with me on his hit list? Regardless, I didn't want him to look up.

Liz made my change, but just as I reached for it, she noticed someone wanted a beer and pulled away. I looked back at Ace. He was squinting at me.

"Hey!" he yelled.

I stared back.

He motioned me over with his hand. "Comere."

Liz held the change out and I took it without looking at her. "Comere," I heard him say again.

I stuffed the bills in my pocket and walked to him. He wrapped his arm around my shoulder. "You know somethin'?" he said.

"Hey, Acc."

"You know somethin'?" he said again.

"No," I shook my head.

"Your daddy and my daddy were best friends."

"They were?"

He nodded emphatically. "Best friends."

"I didn't know that."

"All he talks about."

"About my dad?"

"Best friends."

So our fathers were best friends. In Ace's mind at least. Which is all that matters. Let's leave it at that.

Dad, do you know any Crevans?
Can't say I know anybody by the name of Crevan.
Really?
Not that I can recall. Why?
Doesn't really matter. Just met somebody I thought you might know.

Whether our dads were friends or not, I appreciated the easy slide into friendship with Ace. After that night at Liz's, he never failed to wave or stop by the camp when he was up my way. And he made a point to drop off little things to me that he thought I could use: a piece of two-by-four, the water tank off a mobile home, the butt end of a piling. Like my camp was a larger version of Boo Radley's knothole.

"You never know what you might need," he always said.

Ace's friendship was an unlikely gift. I didn't expect the rest of my friendships to evolve so easily. And there were still many swamp people left that I hadn't gotten through to. Foremost was Butch Dobson.

I came to accept a couple of things that year: it wasn't going to possible to be friends with everybody, and maybe I'd be forced to self-publish some of my books one day. Just to get them off the shelf. Just to have something to show for my time. After all, I'd built the swamp camp. I'd done that. And I'd made a lot of good swamp friends. Surely that was enough.

Big Generator

Gas gets much more expensive, I'm gonna start makin' my own.

You know how to make gas?

Yeah.

How?

Just get you some barrels and some corn. I got books on it at Momma's.

Corn gas?

Yeah.

And you can just pour it in your truck and it runs?

Long as it's sixty-proof. And if you ain't got nowhere to go, you can sit there and drink it.

Crap.

I ain't kiddin' you. I know about a corn heater, too. Dump a bushel of corn in it and it'll go twenty-four hours, droppin' one kernel at a time.

Crap. How much corn does it take to make a gallon of gas?

I can get two and a half gallons a bushel. See that sack over there? That's about a bushel. You can eat it. Bait hogs with it. Make whiskey. Drive your car. I'm like to go all corn if them gas prices don't start droppin'.

Jack, what's the deal with diesel generators? Maybe that's what I need. I want somethin' that's gonna work every time I come up here. I'm tired of this crap."

"Diesel's the way to go."

"I don't know anything about 'em. What's a good one?"

"Get you one like mine."

"That thing's huge. Don't they make somethin' smaller than that?"

"They make 'em. It won't be worth a damn."

" . . . I'd have to build my generator shed bigger. Maybe rewire some stuff. I still get confused over all that 110 and 220."

"I'll help you with it."

"Screw it. You know where I can get one?"

"I got one I'll sell you cheap. Traded my old outboard for it not too long ago."

"How much?"

"Thousand dollars."

"I'll take it."

"Son of a bitch'll run, now."

"You think it'll push both my window units at the same time?"

"That and light up a football field."

I resurrected the pontoon boat for what would be its last trip. I trailered it to where Jack was living on Weeks Bay. He and Carla had divorced, and since then he stayed in his childhood home with his parents. When I turned off the dirt road and pulled into the yard, I saw how Jack had come to know so much about machinery and construction. The place looked like a salvage yard with everything from water pumps to old trucks to sledgehammers and deep freezes. Excitement and awe coursed through me at the sight of this place. It was a man's playground.

Jack stepped out of a screen door onto the porch of the main house, which still stood much in the tradition of an old fishing cottage. It's weird seeing swamp people when you're not in the swamp. You tend to forget that most of them have jobs and real houses. I'll never forget when I ran across Jack in town one time. It was like seeing a deer in Walmart.

"Didn't get lost did you?"

"No," I said out of my truck window. "I didn't have any problems."

Jack looked to his left where an enormous machine stood on the porch. "There she is," he said.

I got out of the truck and approached it. It was a giant, hulking piece of iron machinery mounted on skids and painted army green. It reminded me of something unbolted and robbed from the floor of a factory.

"How we gonna get that thing loaded?" I asked.

"Hold on."

Jack stepped off the porch and walked across the yard to an old wood barn. He disappeared inside and returned shortly with a length of chain. Coursing out through the salvage yard, he climbed onto a rusted-out front-end loader, dropped the chain on the floorboard, and pressed the starter button. Nothing. He climbed down again and retrieved a can of ether from atop a nearby deep freeze. He sprayed it somewhere into the nose of the beast and climbed on again. This time the loader snorted and coughed and cranked.

He drove it to the front porch, lifted the shovel, and worked it slowly over the generator and between the porch columns until I was sure it would go through the front wall. It reminded me of a dinosaur sniffing at the windows.

I helped him chain the generator to the shovel and then he lifted it and backed away, swinging the giant machine before him.

"Where you want it!" he yelled.

"Boat!" I pointed.

He nodded and drove around beside the pontoon boat. He lowered it onto the center while I knelt and watched the trailer flatten its leaf springs.

"Good?" he yelled.

"Sure!"

We unhooked the loader and leaned into the boat on our elbows.

"How much you think it weighs?"

"I don't know. A little heavier than mine."

"It looks it."

"Six, seven hundred pounds maybe."

"Where'd it come from?"

"Pulled it out of a shrimp boat."

"I hope I make it back without this trailer rollin' over on me."

"You'll make it. I hope that boat floats."

"Me, too. It's been a while since we've launched her. You gonna show me how it works once I get it up there?"

"We'll get it workin'."

I got it home after a long, slow drive back to Mobile. The first thing I did was call my brother Reid. I knew he would drool over it.

"Man, you won't believe what I just bought."

"What?"

"Generator from hell. You're gonna love it."

"Diesel?"

"Oh yeah."

"How big?"

"We used a front-end loader to get it on the pontoon boat."

"Damn."

"I know. You gotta see it. When you gonna be back in town?"

"Three weeks."

"You wanna help me get it up there?"

"Sure."

I spent the next several weeks expanding the generator shed and reinforcing the mudsills beneath it. When Reid got leave from his job as a supply boat captain, he met me and our old pontoon boat, the Heckler, on the causeway at eight o'clock on Friday morning. Leaving from there it would be a longer trip than usual, but I'd been planning out the event for weeks. The Heckler was already overloaded and balanced precariously on its trailer. The public ramp on the causeway was in much better shape than the one at Cloverleaf and we'd be taking too many chances with a rough launch. Reid also brought my skiff so that he could sheepdog me on the way up in case the Heckler started sinking. We launched both boats and set out.

It was hard to tell if the Heckler was sinking because the weight of the generator was already pressing most of the pontoons below the surface. It probably looked more like a magic carpet than anything buoyant. Reid kept circling me and inspecting things from the outside while I plowed forward.

It took us close to two hours to make what was usually a twenty-five-minute trip. Then we had to figure out how to get the machine up onto the camp and across the deck to the generator shed. We ended up using a car jack to lift one corner of the generator at a time and chock it high enough to roll a mechanic slide beneath it. Then we secured a come-along to one of the porch columns and winched it up a ramp of boards. Once it was on the deck, we could get behind it and push it along. That is, until one of the wheels on the mechanic slide folded and the whole thing fell over onto its side. It was two o'clock in the afternoon.

We stood there and looked at it without speaking for a few seconds. Finally one of us said, "Crap."

"Did it break anything?"

"Unless that starter's meant to come off like that, it did."

"Crap."

"I know."

We sat down for a while and watched it. Without the mechanic slide we were doomed. We couldn't move it an inch. And the machine was lying on its side on open deck.

"When you gotta get back?" I asked my brother.

"About an hour ago."

"Man, I can't just leave this thing out here. Thousand-dollar bill layin' out for the takin'."

"I doubt it."

"Surely the rain won't help it."

Reid had to leave, but my other brother Murray came up to take a shift. We worked until after dark and finally got the generator standing up again using two-by-four levers. But we couldn't budge it forward at all. "I've got to go find some swamp friends," I said. "I'm dyin'."

We rode over to Mayhall's new camp and were fortunate to find Horace there with three friends. They were all just drunk enough to get excited over the task. They followed us back to my camp, howling at the night. When we arrived, one of them looked up on the deck and said, "Crap."

I said, "I told you."

"Hell," Horace said. "You got a chain?"

"Yeah."

"You got a four-by-four?"

"Yeah."

"Get 'em."

I brought Horace what he needed and he tied the top of the machine to the middle of the four-by-four. Then the four of them, with two on each end, lifted it like a pig on a spit. The middle of the beam was bowing so much I didn't think it would hold. They had about four inches' clearance off the deck and their knees were trembling. As they moved forward, the generator began to sway from side to side, the skids swinging over their ankles. "Man, you guys are—"

But they scuffed along until they had it inside the shop. "Just put it down in there," I told them. "You guys are gonna kill somebody."

It hit the floor and they dropped beam and chain and backed away from it. We stared at it like a fire. "Crap!" somebody said again.

The Dark Ages

I decided to stop writing. Stacked all around my office were drafts of manuscripts I'd spewed out over the last fifteen years. Thirty short stories, ten novels, screenplays, novellas, a few poems. I felt like the last man standing in a quiet battlefield with dead soldiers stacked at my feet.

I didn't know what was good. I didn't know what would sell. I didn't even know who my audience was supposed to be. It was just a bunch of swamp writing. Was I going to grow old and die with this stuff at my feet? Was I a complete fool?

It was obvious that I needed someone to give me direction and focus if I was ever to see any of my material in print. I needed a New York agent. I decided I would stop writing and start submitting to agents until I had one. I was going to submit to every literary agent in New York until one of them took me or I hit the end of the list.

I'd felt discouraged before, but I'd never let rejection get in the way of my writing for long. Now it seemed that I was giving the craft an ultimatum. That bothered me. I was considering giving up if I couldn't get a novel published. I had a growing family and my swamp life to worry about, and nightly toil over words and paper was a time-consuming and selfish occupation that was becoming hard to justify.

"Sometimes I think I might really suck," I told my wife. "Who writes all these novels and doesn't sell even one? Am I a complete fool? How do I know I don't suck?"

"But you're so good."

"But you're my wife and you're supposed to say that. And you don't know how many people there are trying to do just what I'm doing."

"But they can't be writing as much as you."

"Maybe they are. Maybe more. I don't know."

What could she say? My struggle was self-imposed. So I shut down my computer for a long rest and reorganized my office into a mailing center. I took my ninth and tenth novels and sent each of them to five different New York agents. I would do this each month for a year. Then I would quit.

The rejection letters started pouring in. I remained numb to it all. Month after month I let them pile up on my desk while I stuffed more envelopes and crossed out names on my list. And then I'd shut the door to my office and head to the swamp, where the rejection didn't matter.

Once I installed the new diesel generator in the expanded generator shed and replaced the broken starter for three hundred and fifty dollars, it was time to figure out how to make it go. It had been close to three months since I'd seen Jack crank it on the porch of Momma's house, and the camp had been limping along on my old gasoline model that worked about a third of the time. I tried to remember Jack's instructions.

"Pull the crabbing string tied to the throttle and loop it around the screw that sticks out. Twist these two wires together. Flip the compression levers to the left. Turn the key. Flip the compression levers back to the right when it gets some momentum."

A month and four car batteries later, I determined that the source of my problem was something called the solenoid. I'd heard of one. Didn't know what it did. Ordered a new one for sixty dollars and installed it and the beast came to life. I jumped up and down in the generator shed and then walked outside and saw the lightbulbs glowing. I had arrived once again.

The first thing I wanted to do was run both window unit air conditioners at once, something that had never been done at the Swamp Camp without blowing fuses. I stepped into the camp house and flipped the switch. The lights dimmed immediately, and I heard the beast start to cough and drag back in its lair. The air conditioner rattled and blew a little hot breath at me. My stomach knotted.

"Jack, I've got some electrical issues. Man, I need your help. I'm four months into this thing."

"I'll come look at it. We'll get it goin'."

Jack came the next week with a voltmeter and checked it out. "Somethin's wrong," he told me. "We need to get Mayhall."

Mayhall and Jack came the next week with his voltmeter and checked it out. "Somethin's wrong," he told Jack. "It'll run the lights but not much more than that. I think we need to get a generator guy up here."

A month later, at ninety-five dollars an hour, I brought the generator guy up in my boat and he took it apart and looked at it. "Somethin's wrong," he told me. "I think we need to haul it back to Mobile and get it checked out."

I was a beat man. I was headed back to the casino. We unbolted the generator head and muscled it into the boat and back to Cloverleaf. I watched the guy take it away in the back of his truck. Somehow, I knew I wouldn't see it again.

"I can't quit now," I told a friend of mine who owned a business of supply boats. "I'm too deep into this thing."

"How old is it?"

"Old."

"Do they even make parts for it anymore?"

"Sort of. There's some aftermarket guy I can get 'em from that rips me off."

"How much money have you got in it?"

"I'm not gonna say."

"You'd best quit now."

"I can't."

"I know."

My boss said somebody came into the bank and told him, "Bill, I just don't know what to do. Every time I open the door to my restaurant I start losing money."

"I'll tell you what you need to do," my boss said. "I've seen this a hundred times."

"Yeah?"

"You go back to your restaurant right now and close the door."

Airboat

Jack, how fast you think your airboat'll go?
I don't know. Old boy I bought it from said he didn't even need wa-
ter. Said he could drive it right up the ramp and up the road to
his house.

I liken Jack's airboat to a magnolia leaf with an airplane prop attached. He sits on the high chair directly in front of the propeller cage
and patiently waits for his passengers to climb in, grab some ear protection off the floor, and hold onto the bars at the side of the bench
seat below him. Once you're facing forward, I imagine he smiles with
mischief.

The purpose of an airboat is to go places in the swamp where you
don't think you should be able to go. With the deafening noise of the
airplane engine and the concentration it takes to hold onto the seat,
the experience is very individual.

I can remember clearly the first time I felt the engine throbbing
beneath me like I was riding a Harley—because half of the boat is
engine, and one simply sits on a thin metal seat in front of the thun-
derous machine. It was pitch-dark and Jack switched on the floodlights and Chuckfee Bay lay before us like the salt flats of Utah. He
eased down on the throttle and we surged forward into the night. Little patches of fog sat on the water, and we passed in and out of these,

blind and then seeing the water again, my hair wet and plastered against my face. Then suddenly we hit the opposite side of the bay, a savanna of swamp grass that I'd gazed over many times and wondered about. The boat hopped a little onto its new plain and then we were swishing along again like it was nothing but water beneath us. I heard a faint "hold on" and I gripped my seat tighter. Then the airboat was going sideways and then in a circle and then straight again. I turned to look at Jack. He tried not to smile, but he couldn't help himself.

I twirled my finger in the air. "Again," I mouthed.

As dangerous as it feels to be in Jack's airboat, I've found it can be more dangerous to be out of it.

I've admitted to some that Crazy Dan had me out in the swamp one night looking for a coatimundi. I'm not proud of falling for that bit of mischief, but I'm grateful that I survived. While I sometimes joke about the prank, I don't often talk about how the night ended.

By midnight we were sitting in his old walk-through bow rider that he'd salvaged from somewhere, resting and floating about fifty yards inside the mouth of Chicory Creek. I was worn out from the coatimundi search, but Dan was still listening for one, whatever they sound like.

In the distance we heard Jack and his airboat, buzzing the marsh like a runaway chainsaw. A mile away in the other direction I heard several gunshots. The swamp people were all out that night with their particular flavor of entertainment. Somehow I'd ended up on a date with Crazy Dan.

"Forget about it, Dan," I said. "I'm done."

"Shhh," he said.

I thought about how much I wanted to be in bed. I vaguely realized there was no coatimundi and I was too tired to care. The sound of Jack's airboat grew louder like a mosquito finally finding my ear.

"Dan?"

"Shhh," he said.

I looked in the direction of Chuckfee Bay, but all I saw was a wall of swamp grass. We'd drifted around a bend in the creek to a place where the boat was hidden in the cattails and buggy whips. Then I thought about Jack always wanting to cut the corners.

"You got any lights on this thing, Dan?"

He didn't answer me.

Suddenly floodlights passed overhead, lighting the top of the marsh grass.

"Jesus, Dan, he's coming up the creek!"

Dan didn't shush me, but he showed zero concern about our predicament. I realized there was no time to start his boat and really nowhere safe to go if we did. I heard the airboat roar and charge the mouth of the creek. *There's no way he can see us,* I thought. *He's going right over the top of us, crushing the boat and ramping himself to swamp Heaven.*

I dove to the floor just as I saw the grass begin to shudder. Dan cocked his head and studied the trees like he'd heard something strange.

Jack noticed us at the last second and swerved. I saw the bottom of the airboat tilted up and rising beside us like a black wall. His wake rocked us against the creek bank.

I sat up. Dan turned in his seat and studied the airboat while Jack pulled to a stop and shut it off.

"What y'all up to?" Jack asked.

Crazy Dan brought a finger to his lips. "Shhh," he said.

Where's the airboat?

Gettin' fixed.

What happened to it?

You didn't hear about it?

No.

I sunk it out there in Raft.

How deep?

I know my ears were poppin' when I had to swim down and tie a rope to it. Must be twenty feet to the mud.

How'd it happen?

We had a big alligator lyin' in the boat with us. About four of us. This old boy said, "You wanna see how you make an alligator mad?" Before I could stop him, he hauls off and kicks it in the head. That son of a bitch jumps up hissin' with his mouth open. Everybody ran to the bow and that boat dipped and went down so fast that I felt it hit bottom before I could get my hand off the throttle.

Anybody get hurt?

Naw. We all popped up. We come up later with some come-alongs and pulled it out. It weren't easy.

Crap.

Them things'll sink, now.

I stopped off at a fellow's camp one afternoon late when I saw a few boats that I recognized tied out front. They were sitting on the porch drinking Miller High Life and talking about the previous nights' escapades.

One of them says, "You remember that night you swam out there naked with that knife in your teeth and cut that fellah's bow rope? It must have been twenty degrees that night."

I thought back to a story I'd heard years before.

The Phone Call

September 2004. Katie contacted me at work. "I just got a phone call from an agent in New York. She wants you to call her back. She talked to me for almost thirty minutes asking me all these questions."

"What? Like what questions?"

"Like how long had you been writing and how many books had you written."

"You tell her?"

"I told her you had all this stuff and how you'd been writing every night since we'd been married and—"

"Hell, since before that."

"Well, she said she could tell you were a real writer."

"She said that? What's her name? Who's she with?"

It had taken ten months. I had finally reached a New York literary agent. I called her back that afternoon with trembling hands. She wanted to represent me. A contract was in the mail.

Three days later I got a call from another literary agent. She wanted to represent me too. All those years and suddenly two agents within three days. *Alabama Moon* had broken through the big wall.

I did my research and chose between the two agents based on the sales record of their agency. In reality, finding representation is only half the fight. They still have to sell your book to an editor at a publishing house. And they have many projects that don't sell. Just like realtors can't always sell a house. But I was closer than I'd ever been. I finally had a voice in the publishing world who believed in what I was doing and had the connections to introduce me to the editors.

"I'm going to submit your novel to three publishers," my agent told me. "We should know something in a couple of months."

Three, I thought. *That's all?* I was used to the shotgun approach. And when she told me the names of the publishers she was submitting to, even more water was thrown on the fire of my optimism.

"I've already sent *Alabama Moon* to all those places," I said.

She was unmoved. "That's fine," she said. "I'm sure you didn't get it to the right people."

I was doubtful but willing to go along with whatever plan she had. It was a tremendous weight off me to know that for the first time in fifteen years I could sit back, breathe, and relax with good conscience.

Jack, what's goin' on?

Not much, man. You headed up there?

In about an hour ago.

I heard that.

Where are you?

Home Depot. I'll be up later on.

Come see me.

I'll be over there. You get that generator runnin'?

No.

We'll get you another one.

Man, you don't have to do that. I probly screwed it up when I rolled it or wired it wrong or somethin'.

We'll get you another one.

I don't know if I can live through another one. I'm thinkin' I might not be cut out for a diesel.

I'll help you.

Well, I've got this cheap gas one I brought up and it won't push

everything I need, but it's nice to have power again.
I feel bad about that other.
Well, don't.
I'm gonna set things right.
Just get up here and drink some beer with me.

Jack, there's not much to this Miller High Life Light.
Ain't as much as what's in the other.

Where'd you get this pottery?
Over there in Oak Bayou. It's all over them shell mounds.
Indian pottery?
Yeah. I ever show you the jawbone I found with the big tooth?
No.
Check it out. They gonna have to carbon 409 this son of a bitch.
What the hell is that?
Looks like a big panther or somethin'.
But there's a molar behind it. Do cats have molars?
I don't know. Whatever it is, them Indians killed it and ate it, or it
    them, one.

I think I'm gonna stick with this bottle of Miller High Life.
Ain't nothin' like a tall blonde.

I didn't write a word. I didn't mail a thing. I went to the camp and drank beer with Jack and the boys. One cool fall afternoon I motored deep into Chicory Bayou alone. I stripped down to my underwear and lay on my stomach across the bow. I stared down at the clear water and the waving swamp grass. I floated down the creek like that for an hour, watching the bass and bream suspended in the peaceful depths.

Back to the Mud

How you doin', Ace?

Whoa, son, we been hittin' it.

You feelin' pretty good?

Me an' Johnny Walker.

Yeah. I'm gonna be up for a couple of days. You stayin' up for a while?

I might come back tonight. Listen, you need anything, you let me know. I got pieces of six-by-six, got some two-by-fours. I just haul up a little piece here and there. You never know what you might need. You just let me know.

Thanks, I will.

That was the last conversation I had with Ace. I heard that he finally caught up with his ex-wife's lover and had to leave town over whatever happened. Then I heard he was back in town training to build electrical control boards. Then he was gone again. No one knew where he was. Regardless, he was not in the delta, and his camp started to sag and lean even more. On breezy nights I heard the roof tin tapping and slowly working its way loose. Once the roof goes, the rest is not far behind. The swamp comes at it from all directions.

Having to watch Ace's camp deteriorate only fueled my fears of losing my own camp. And I knew it wasn't only the fear of actually losing

my camp but of seeing all that effort, all those good times, going to the mud.

To add more weight to my worries, it had been two months since I'd heard from my New York agent. It had been nice to bury my head in the sand for a while, but the slow creep of reality was starting to get me in the gut. I was expecting the call any day.

"We couldn't sell it," they'd say.

If I got that phone call, my writing pursuits were over. I just couldn't go through all that again. There comes a time when reason gets heavier than passion or goals or whatever it is you call it.

If I could just keep my swamp camp. . . . At least then I would have *something*. Something I'd made that I was proud of. That would be out there and last. That I could show to my kids and say, "That's me. That's what I'm all about."

But the lease on my land was a never-ending tangle of family disputes and uncertainty. It was clear they wanted to sell it all, and it was only a matter of time before I'd have to leave my camp. Let it go back to the mud like it never was.

"I need to buy some land up here," I told Jack. "I need to own my camp. Then I won't have to worry about all this."

Jack was sweating it out, too. I wasn't sure what his plan was. I don't think he had one.

"I tell you about that old boy across the bay?" he said.

"No. What old boy?"

"Pam and that girlfriend of little Mayhall's was checkin' catfish lines one mornin' after I'd gone to work. They said they drove up in that creek and seen his boat sunk and his cooler floatin' in the water and full beer cans strung out in a little line with the current. They look up in that camp and he's all balled up in his tent. It was hotter'n hell that afternoon."

"What was wrong with him?"

"They start yellin' up at him and he ain't movin'. Finally they call the Coast Guard and the marine police. They figure he's up in there dead. One of 'em eventually gets out of the boat and walks up to the doorway and looks closer at him. He jumps up and yells, 'What the hell you want?'"

"Pam and that old girl tell him they thought he was dead and called the Coast Guard and the marine police. He starts scrapin' around for his clothes, hollerin', 'What the hell'd you do that for?'"

I immediately saw what Jack was getting at.

"You think he'd sell his camp to me?" I asked.

"He needs to sell it to somebody. I know I don't have the money."

"I don't have much either, but I'll borrow it if I have to."

"Ride over there and check it out."

The camp was built on the first of several twenty-five-foot lots that had been carved out and sold a few years before. I remember seeing a for sale sign and calling about them. They'd wanted seven thousand dollars apiece and I just couldn't see paying that kind of money for swampland. I'd regretted that decision many times since.

It was framed and roofed, windows and doors in, but no siding. Just black plastic tarp half stapled to the studs. So leaky that the man had pitched a tent in it.

No one was home that day and the black plastic flapped in the breeze. It was the most depressing, nightmarish place one could ever spend a night. But I kept trying to get my head around the structure, trying to find some redeeming qualities. Nothing was square and the whole thing was chocked and propped out of the mud like he could never stop it from sinking. Pieces of untreated plywood lay across the mud like a gangplank and a paint-specked aluminum ladder was the only way up.

I tried to ignore the camp and value the lot. Although it was narrow, it had deepwater access on the creek that fronted it. The view to the south encompassed all of Chuckfee Bay. It was a great place to have a drink and watch the sun set.

I kept driving by the place on weekends, hoping to meet the owner. One day I saw people sitting on the porch of the camp next door. I stopped and asked them if they knew their neighbor.

"Yeah," they said. "He's in here."

After a second, this man in his early sixties shuffled onto the porch.

"What do you want?"

"I was wonderin' if your camp was for sale."

"I'll sell it to you."

"How much?"

The price was exorbitant for a tiny piece of swampland, but I'd have paid twice what he asked. He climbed down off the porch while I tied my boat to the creek bank. We met in front of his place and introduced ourselves. He said his name was Walter Smith.

"It'd be a good buy," he said to me. "You've got state land on this side of you and won't nobody ever build over there. And my camp comes with it. I've still got a little bit of work to do, but it's mostly done. That's my ex-son-in-law next door. He's a good guy. I usually hang out with him when I'm up."

I studied the camp. I had never seen such a chocked-up and canti-levered support system. One corner of the place was still held up by an old railroad jack. Walter saw me looking at it.

"And that jack'll come with it, too," he added.

I nodded.

"You can get up in there if you want."

"That's okay."

"You wanna walk around it?"

I didn't see the need. The whole place would have to be torn down. But I walked around it anyway just to make Walter feel better. He was proud of the place, a feeling I understood.

Before I left, we traded contact information and I told him I'd be in touch.

I thought about things for a few days. I also sketched out plans for a new camp that would fit the dimensions of the lot. I got everything worked out except for the money. It was a bad time for me financially. Christmas was coming and taxes were due, not to mention an endless list of expenses that I felt should take priority.

But I couldn't walk away.

I called Walter and offered him five hundred dollars to give me a one-year option to work it out.

The Deal

In late November my agent forwarded an email to me one morning at the office. It was an offer for *Alabama Moon*. With the click of a mouse fifteen years of my work were suddenly validated. I had never worked so hard for anything. It was the happiest day of my life.

"Do you want to accept it?" she asked me.

"Why wouldn't I?"

"We may be able to get more money if we wait for additional offers."

I would have given it to them for free. "Take it," I said. "I don't want to screw this up."

"I think that's wise," she agreed. "It's a fair offer."

There were still some minor contractual details to work out, but my agent said I shouldn't be worried. She notified the publisher that we accepted the offer. That afternoon the editor at the publishing house called to congratulate me and discuss the novel.

"When do I come to New York and sign something?" I asked, impulsively adding the g's to my words.

"There's no reason to come up here. We FedEx everything to you."

"I've just always imagined that I'd get to come to New York and sign something."

All of those years I'd had an image of walking down a tall, long, white marble hall between oil paintings of great writers, like a president touring the White House for the first time. Faulkner, Steinbeck,

Hemingway. Then a crusty, powerful editor and a giant mahogany desk and a fountain pen made of an eagle feather.

"Well," the editor continued, "we don't really work that way. I don't even handle the contracts. I'm sorry."

"I've just always had it in my head how it was going to be. I've always wanted to sign something."

He didn't reply.

"I'm coming to New York," I said. "I don't care what I sign. It can be a blank piece of paper."

Katie and I went to New York a few weeks later. There were no marble halls or oil paintings. The publishing house was a real business and people had offices that were no bigger than my own. They didn't wear suits and the editors answered their own phones. I'm not saying that I was any less impressed. I felt like someone going to pick up their lottery check and finding that it's a hundred million instead of a hundred and fifty million dollars.

One moment stands out in my mind more than others. I was sitting in my editor's office, soaking up the feeling of finally being there. His floor was covered with stacks of manuscripts, and he showed me a few that were promising and others that weren't going to make it. At one point he opened his top desk drawer and pulled out a stack of postcard-size forms and asked me if I'd seen one before. He was enjoying himself. I knew exactly what they were. I'd been getting those cold, tear-out rejection slips for years.

He took a phone call and gave me time to gaze around his office. Behind my chair was a wall of bookshelves with stacks of manuscripts. Beneath each stack was a label with an author's name. I saw my name was beneath a short stack and I turned back to him and pointed at it.

"I've got my own shelf space?" I said.

He nodded at me and smiled with the phone to his ear.

While he finished his conversation, I began to think back on all the failures I'd had over the years. I turned away from the shelf with my name on it and took a deep breath and regained composure. Surely there was yet another hurdle somewhere that I would have to jump before I could actually see my book in print.

He hung up the phone. "So," I said. "Is this like the movie business? Do you buy a bunch of manuscripts each year and then sit at a round table and decide which ones to print?"

"No, we publish every book we buy. It's in your contract that we have to print it."

"Well, then you have to sell it, right? What if the bookstores don't want it?"

The editor smiled. He was enjoying himself again. "The bookstores usually buy all of our books."

"So there is no way that my book won't be in a bookstore in Mobile, Alabama?"

"Watt."

"Yeah."

"Relax. You made it."

And so I had.

More Hurricanes

In September 2004, Hurricane Ivan raced over the Gulf Coast. The tidal surge wiped out most marine structures on Mobile Bay, but up in the delta, the swamp calmed and absorbed it so that the camps escaped with only a little water on the floor.

Katrina hit the next year. My generation had never seen anything like it.

Before both storms I recruited help to secure the camp. Just as had happened with Hurricane Georges, the river was high and calm and rippled with an unusual south wind. People talk about how unfortunate civilization was before storm technology, how they must have been caught off guard by these hurricanes. To a certain extent, I agree with them. But there is no mistaking the day before a hurricane arrives, even under blue skies. Nature is completely calm, eerie, like something at the gallows. For lack of a more precise word, the air and the water and the birds and clouds are just weird. A treacherous and deadly force is marching toward you from hundreds of miles away and you can almost hear the drumbeat of it.

Katrina dealt a death blow to the Mississippi coast. It hit with the intensity that only those who had been through Hurricane Camille in the late 1960s could comprehend. The force of it extended all the way into Alabama and thrashed us worse than any other direct hit I'd seen. Suddenly I understood the washed-over shell banks where old creosote pilings lay stripped and rotting—all that was left of a bygone generation of camps.

Just about every camp on the river was washed away like a stick hut. Houseboats were in the trees. Dead animals were everywhere. The water was littered with debris, and the rivers ran like sewage seeps in a Third World country.

But my camp remained standing with most of the others on the south bank of Chuckfee Bay. All that had saved us was the island of hackberry and marsh between the bay and Raft River to the south. It had acted as a giant filter to break up the violence.

I lost some of the roof. The inside of the camp was coated with mud. Water had risen five feet into the main room, almost to the top of the door. All of the furniture was ruined. The amount of work to be done was overwhelming. I wasn't sure if the camp would ever be the same.

Sissy's brother went up there durin' the hurricane and said he found a little hill where they was all gathered up. Came back with twenty-eight hogs in his boat.

Twenty-eight!

You got-damn right. Said they was herded up on that island—deer and hogs and coons and God knows what else.

Durin' the hurricane.

Hell yeah. That boy's crazy.

You see Hodgson's little camp?

No.

Looks like somethin' chewed it up and spit it about a half mile upriver. All up in the trees.

Damn.

That fellow can't get a break.

For a couple of weeks, I did nothing. The job that faced me was daunting.

Finally I began to formulate a plan. The first thing I had to do was carry every piece of furniture out of the swamp. I called all of the camp members and asked each of them to make a trip up and get a boatload of stuff and haul it to a landfill somewhere. I came up with a guy from work and pulled everything out and stacked it on the porch. Over the next month, the pile started slowly disappearing.

After all of the debris had been hauled away, I called the members and set a date for a work party. This might have been the first work party ever at the swamp camp. Many of the members didn't use the place, and I'd always felt guilty about requiring anyone to help out with something they didn't use. But if we were to get it back in shape again, I'd need all the help I could get.

I was surprised that so many showed up for the event. And I'd been so used to doing everything myself that it was amazing to me how much we got done. Using shop-vacs and an electric pump with a garden hose attached, several people washed and vacuumed out all of the mud. I got up on the roof and replaced the missing sheet tin. The others collected and sacked the remaining wet stuff. In a day, we had the whole place cleaned out and the roof repaired.

People began donating new furniture and appliances, and I hauled them up over the next few weeks. Things slowly came back together again.

Man, that crappy camp on Sand's still there!
Must have played dead on the hurricane.

It was a while before I was able to cross the bay and check on Walter's camp. I thought that surely it had been scattered like a straw house. But when I turned into Sand Bayou, there it was. The storm had destroyed just about every other camp around him, but his sat there mocking me, looking just as I remembered it.

Just buy it, I thought. *Time is running out. Borrow the money. Do what you have to do.*

Stepping Out

In six months, *Alabama Moon* would be in bookstores. I still hadn't told any of my swamp friends about it. One night over a few drinks I decided to come clean. Jack was my friend and I felt like a fraud and a spy, sitting there soaking up all of his stories and arcane swamp lore to use for my benefit.

"Jack, you know I'm a writer."

"I heard somethin' about that."

"You did? How?"

"We figured you was up to somethin' over there all these years."

"I'm serious. Like New York and all that."

"I got some stories, now."

"I know you do. Most everything good I've got you told me."

"You gonna get rich?"

"No, but I'll get this stuff printed. I just don't know how I can tell it all without gettin' people mad at me. I don't want anybody burnin' down my swamp camp."

"They ain't gonna burn you."

"They burned Hargett."

"They ain't gonna burn you."

I reasoned Jack wasn't forecasting, he was offering assistance.

"These New York people said they want to come down here," I continued.

"We'll show 'em a good time."

"You think you could take 'em out in your airboat?"

"We'll take 'em out. Get 'em down here."

My optimism was overflowing. "I wanna build a swamp lodge one day, Jack. Get people to pay by the night. Like a bed and breakfast."

"You could do it."

"But I'd need to own the land. I need to find a piece of this swamp-land for sale and buy it. I'll build the lodge and maybe you can be the tour guide."

"We'll set it up."

"I'm serious, man. One day when I'm a full-time writer. Like when I'm fifty or somethin'. It'd just need to break even. I could make the rest writin' books."

Jack shifted and I could tell he was interested.

"I got the airboat," he said. "We could do some frog hunts. Catch some gators."

"They'd love all that stuff. Catfish traps, jugs, hog hunts."

"Get 'em down here."

"Nobody's ever tried that out here. I'll bet people would pay for that. I'll bet it would go."

But I doubt Jack took me seriously. People like him had issues more important than speculating about a break-even swamp bed and breakfast. Jack's recent divorce had left him stripped of just about everything he'd accumulated since he'd been married, which wasn't a wealthy man's load to begin with. And now he was living at his momma's and in between jobs. His main concern was making enough money to buy beer and keep his engines running. Man talk, all of it.

A few months before *Alabama Moon* came out, the *Mobile Register* asked if they could write an article on me that would print near the release date. They wanted to publish a brief bio accompanied by photos of me at the swamp camp.

I took off work early one afternoon and met the reporter and photographer at Cloverleaf. Fortunately the place was deserted and no one was there to ask what we were up to. Even though Jack was now in the know about my writing, I doubted he'd talked to anyone about it. But reporters in the delta usually meant trouble to swamp camps with all of the questionable building code violations and environmental practices.

We loaded quite a bit more gear than I'd imagined into my boat and headed out. Once we arrived at the camp and began to set up, the equipment came out of the cases and unfolded and telescoped into even more. Lighting devices and umbrella-like backdrops made quite a display on the porch of the camp. As I moved about for various setups, I kept an eye cocked at the bay for any sign that my swamp friends had caught me in such a vain act.

To my relief, we were able to finish and head back without being discovered. But over the next few weeks, the thought of that article coming out bothered me. I was going to be on the front page of the Living section, claiming to be the Swamp Writer. A self-proclaimed delta expert. All of this when I still felt like a wide-eyed kid around my swamp friends. In reality, if you took a helicopter and buzzed it over the delta and corralled all of the swamp people like gazelles on the African savanna, I would probably be branded in the corral with a C+. Butch Dobson was going to get a laugh. I hoped.

Big Generator 2

Jack made good on his promise to get another diesel generator for me. Even though I was up and running with my new gasoline model, there was still a faint glimmer of hope that I would eventually have a big diesel like the other swamp people.

"I got it ready for you."

"At your momma's?"

"Yeah."

"All right. I'll be over there Saturday to pick it up in my truck."

"We can load it in your boat and run it up there."

"Man, I'm gonna have to rest a while longer before I get into that again. I'll just bring it back home and work on it in the yard and get it ready."

"It's ready."

"You don't think it needs any new parts?"

"Maybe a new on-off switch and the starter falls off sometimes. Just needs a bolt in it. Might need to drain out the oil and change some filters and stuff. Maybe rewire some of the plugs on it."

"Okay . . . I think I'll still let it rest in the yard for a while."

"Suit yourself. I'll see you Saturday."

This new one was a factory green Onan stabled out among the other machinery in his momma's yard. Jack got the front-end loader cranked and lifted it out and set it in my truck. I watched my tires

sink up into the wheel wells and wondered how I was going to ever unload it.

"I think this one's bigger, Jack."

"Little bit."

"Maybe a lot bigger."

"It'll fire some stuff up."

"Where'd you get it?"

"I traded some more stuff for it."

We leaned into the truck bed and Jack pointed at different places on the machine, describing what made it work. He showed me the missing bolt that caused the starter to fall off and waved his hands around the area where I needed to replace the electrical outlets. My brain raced and jerked, trying to note everything I had to remember.

It took me nearly two hours of white-knuckle driving to get home. All that time I couldn't figure out how I was going to get it out of my truck, much less into a boat and up to the camp. I really just wanted to leave it in the yard for some sense of closure.

I drove across the lawn with my three excited kids trailing "Daddy's big surprise." I drove to the back fence and saw a solution. With the children watching I draped a rope over my shoulder and started climbing an old white oak. It had been a long time since I'd climbed a tree, and each time I stopped to look down, my legs trembled.

"Don't fall, Daddy," my oldest daughter yelled up at me.

"I'm not," I said.

I reached the limb I was going for and dropped the rope over so that both ends touched the ground. I returned to earth and fastened a come-along to another tree. Then I tied one end of the rope to the come-along and the other end to the generator. My plan was to drive out from under the machine and leave it swinging from the limb above. Then I could lower it gently to the ground with the hand winch.

"Stand back, kids."

They knew those words usually meant a loud tool was about to start or something violent was going to happen. The kids scattered across the yard to a healthy distance. I cranked the truck and eased forward. The rope grew taut and the generator began to slide backward in small jerks. Finally it tipped off the tailgate and dropped like a Sherman tank, uprooting the oak and bringing the tree crashing down over the back of my pickup. The kids cheered. I drove out from under it all, got out, and left the generator buried beneath the tree canopy. Where it still sits to this day.

Famous

A*labama Moon* hit the bookshelves on September 5, 2006. That week I was interviewed on local television morning shows, spoke at conferences and schools, and of course, was on the front page of the Living section standing on the porch of the camp. My phone was ringing with people wanting to congratulate me and emails and letters began to trickle in. I was busier than I'd ever been in my life, making appearances and corresponding and holding my day job at the same time. Certainly too busy to keep up my routine of spending nights in the swamp.

September moved into October and the camp stood empty. Fall is the prettiest time of year in the swamp, and I thought about it all the while I was driving through the South to promote the book. The water was mirror calm and the breezes cool. Jack and the boys were up there setting catfish traps and catching speckle trout. There were some new camps going up to replace those that had been swept away by Hurricane Katrina. Carson had probably finished the new equipment shed he was building near the riverbank. My boat lapped gently in its slip under the tin roof I'd built with Connor those years back. I missed all of these things.

I seemed to understand how this new attention was going to affect my life in the real world, but what would it be like when I went back to the swamp camp? I wondered how they would treat me. I really just wanted to be Watt. Or did I? What had I worked fifteen years to get?

In the middle of October I had a break in my schedule and left for the swamp. I felt like I was sneaking into the place. At Cloverleaf, I spoke with Carson and Sissy, studying their faces, wondering if they knew anything about my book. They didn't bring it up, and I assumed they didn't. In some ways it was a relief, but in another way I felt like I was keeping secrets from friends again.

Another buddy, Craig, met me at the camp that evening and we cooked steaks and drank whiskey. For a few hours all that other stuff in my life was drowned out and I was back at my favorite place in the world and just me with a hammer and a stack of boards out back. I was just Watt.

About ten o'clock we heard a boat outside. "Hey, Watt!"

I stepped out onto the porch and saw Jack in his boat with another person. "What's up, Jack?"

"We got a book signin' goin' on over at my camp."

"A book signin'?"

"Damn right."

"You're kiddin', right?"

"Got it set up over there," he said.

"You think I'm gonna believe somebody's got a book out here?"

"Get in your boat and come on down."

I turned to Craig. "You might wanna hang out here. There's no tellin' what they're talkin' about."

"I'll get my jacket," he said. "I wouldn't miss this for anything."

We motored to Jack's camp and tied up. I saw several people sitting in the porch light, drinking beer. Jack walked up the dock with us and ushered us into the crowd. "Introduce yourself," he said.

"I'm Watt Key," I said to a young woman sitting on a cooler.

She stood up. "The writer?"

"Yeah," I said, feeling a little presumptuous for saying it. Even though I was now officially a professional writer, I still didn't think of myself that way. My day job was still working with computers.

Her husband and another couple came into the light and introduced themselves and shook my hand. Their glazed-over look may have resulted from other things besides just meeting me. But we began talking and the situation soon became clear. Jack had told his guests that he knew somebody famous just down the riverbank. They had no idea who I was or what my book was called, just that I was the famous author a few camps down—famous because Jack said so. And the more they partied, the more famous I got. Until Jack had to go get me and bring me over.

It wasn't long before the woman was digging around inside Jack's camp for something I could sign for her. Finally she walked into the bathroom, ripped off some toilet paper, and brought it back to me.

"You got a pen?" I asked her.

There was no pen, but we found a construction pencil. She sat across from me at Jack's little kitchen table with her head swaying and her eyes glazed over, having me scrape and tear the names of her children and cousins onto the toilet paper.

"You just don't know how much this means to me," she kept saying.

"I don't mind at all."

"Make one out for my son, Johnny."

"Okay."

"What's the name of the book?"

"*Alabama Moon.*"

"Can you put that on there?"

"Okay."

"I'm gonna get it and read it."

"I appreciate it."

She took Johnny's paper and stuffed it into her jeans pocket. "And make one out to his cousin, James."

"Okay. . . . This one got a little torn. You want me to do it over?"

She looked at it, shook her head, and stuffed it into the pocket with the other one. After I'd signed to several children and relatives, Jack came inside. "Thought I was gonna have to come in here and break you two up."

"Well, Jack, there's certain things that come with bein' famous."

Watch out for them frogs.
She scared of frogs?
I don't know. Just sounded good.

Christmas Gift

.

December in the delta can be windswept, cold, and lonely. At times this is exactly what I'm looking for. During the Christmas holidays I went up to the swamp camp for a night of solitude, hoping to get some work done on a writing project. I was a real author now with contracts and deadlines.

That night I listened to the north wind howling over the camp, rattling the tin on my roof. I woke the next morning to find the water blown out of the swamp and my boat sitting on an ice-coated mud flat. Usually I find a solution to all the inconveniences that arise at the camp, but this situation left me dumbfounded.

I sucked up my pride and called for help.

"Jack, I'm in trouble."

"You on mud?"

"Yeah."

"I'm at work right now. Call Butch. He'll get you out."

"You think he's up here?"

"He's up there."

I'd passed Butch's camp the day before and it had looked deserted. But I should have known better. Butch was always in the swamp, even when you didn't think he was.

"I don't know him real well," I said.

"He's all right."

Jack, master of the understatement, calling someone "all right" was a healthy endorsement. But then again, this was Butch we were talking about. Bottom line, he still intimidated me. After all the years I'd put in with swamp people, he alone remained strangely ambivalent to my presence. Even though I'd made annual stops to visit him, I doubted he even knew my name.

But I saw no other option. Jack gave me his cell number and I called.

"Yeah," he answered.

"Uh, Butch, this is Watt Key. You know—"

"I know who you are."

"I'm up here—"

"I saw you last night."

"Well, my boat's—"

"I figured."

Silence.

"You think you could help me?"

He didn't answer right away. "Start walkin' out to the point," he finally said. "I'll pick you up."

"What about my boat?"

"You wanna watch it or get home?"

"Okay," I said. "I'll see you in a minute."

I trudged through the frozen swamp to a point of land that edged a deep part of the river. Butch was already there in his beat-up aluminum jon boat, blue jeans, and rubber boots, the icy wind whipping the short sleeves of his T-shirt. He studied me from under a stained ball cap pulled down almost over his eyes.

"I really appreciate this," I said.

"Climb in," he mumbled.

On the ride to his camp my mind raced to find appropriate payment for the rescue. I didn't have much cash on me, which was going to make it awkward. And I wasn't sure paying him wouldn't be offensive.

Before I had time to offer him anything, Butch docked at his camp, climbed out of the boat, and shoved me off. "Go ahead and take it in," he said. "Just leave it at the landin'."

"How you gonna get back?"

"I got some boys comin' up in a couple of days. They'll bring it to me."

"You sure about that?"

"Go on," he said.

I didn't know if he was being overly generous or just annoyed with me. But again, I didn't see any options.

"I'll make it up to you," I said.

"Don't worry about it," he said. "Get out of here."

For a few days after that incident I struggled with how I was going to repay Butch. I finally decided to send him a copy of *Alabama Moon* with a letter of thanks written on the title page. If he read it, which I doubted he would, I would have found a way to indirectly introduce myself to him.

Weeks passed after I mailed the book, during which I never saw or heard from Butch. I imagined him looking disgusted at my offering and dropping it in the trash.

A few more weeks passed and my second novel, *Dirt Road Home,* was released. I had the kickoff party one evening at Page and Palette in Fairhope. I was stationed at a table doing my best to keep up with a line of people, trying to put names to familiar faces, talking to them while I'm writing, worried I'm going to misspell something. All that noise and confusion went mute when I glanced up to see a man approaching me in line. He wore jeans and a T-shirt, ball cap pulled low over his eyes, as out of place in this crisp bookstore as a farmer at Churchill Downs.

It made my night. I couldn't have cared if he was the only person in the room.

"Butch," I said.

He bashfully set his copy of *Dirt Road Home* on the table before me.

"Hey, man," he said. "I've only liked one book in my life. *Alabama Moon.* I hope this one's as good."

End of an Era

Over the years I made lots of friends in the swamp. Now, no longer the new boy, I'd even outlasted some of them. Many of my friends were gone, and I was starting to wonder just how long it would last for *me*.

In 2011 Butch and his brother drowned in a boating accident. I subsequently published the previous story, "Christmas Gift," in *Mobile Bay Magazine.* I was not surprised by how many people it affected. Butch's hunting buddies hung the article in his camp. I even got a phone call from his mother.

"He always talked about you," she told me. "He called you Alabama Moon. I never knew your real name."

Ace was gone. Crazy Dan was gone. Horace was gone. Some new people I didn't know had moved in three doors down from me. Almost all of my original camp members had stopped coming up. It was mostly me and my kids and their friends now.

"In the end it all goes back to the mud," an old swamper told me.

I thought about that statement a lot. Ace's camp was starting to sag and lean. On breezy nights I heard the roof tin tapping and slowly working its way loose. Once the roof goes, the rest is not far behind. The swamp comes at it from all directions.

Having to watch Ace's camp deteriorate wasn't the only thing getting me down. For sale signs were up on the property and it was inevitable that I was going to lose my lease when its term was up. Environmental restrictions and a general scarcity of private land in the delta made buying another location difficult. It seemed like an era was coming to an end.

> *You know, I'm gonna buy that piece of property. I went by there this mornin' with Reid. I don't know why I'm draggin' my feet on it.*
> *I saw that old boy a couple of days ago. I was sittin' in here lookin' out the window and I seen him polin' around out there checkin' some crab traps. Spud come in here the next day and said Jimmy's all worked up about somebody runnin' his crab traps. I told him I'd seen that old boy out there. I probably shouldn't have said that. Poor fellow.*

I've been going into the swamps of the Mobile-Tensaw Delta for nearly twenty years. I built a camp, made friends with the swamp people, and wrote about it. Now my own camp is sagging and the tin roof is starting to leak and tap against the north wind. There are water stains on the ceiling and the deck boards seem to rot faster than I can replace them. All those years back I couldn't have imagined that my camp would one day be so worn and full of memories.

This is definitely the end of a major chapter in my life. I can't imagine having to build another camp now, board by board, every weekend for a year. And I no longer have the time, the energy, or the enthusiastic young friends to help me repair the place. It is slowly going back to the mud as I was told it would.

But it's not over. Maybe this camp, maybe this chapter, but not my time out here. I bought the property from Mr. Smith. I plan to tear down the crooked camp and build a new one with my son and his friends. A few years from now when he's a little older and can take over the heavy lifting. I plan to teach him all the things I was taught by my swamp friends. And I plan to sit back and observe and write more stories.

It's already built in my head. I look around my yard. The diesel generator is still where I left it, waiting for a home. My storage shed is full of the scrap lumber I've been saving and the used window units and my mud tools—my man tools. Everywhere I look sit fresh paint and supplies.

And yes, even this new camp will go back to the mud in the end. What doesn't? But over the years I've realized it's not about the camp itself or the book deals. It's about the friendships and the memories. They'd outlast it all.